D1569871

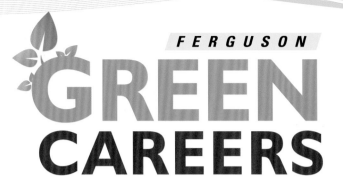

FERGUSON
GREEN
CAREERS

ENVIRONMENT &
NATURAL RESOURCES

FERGUSON

GREEN
CAREERS

ENVIRONMENT &
NATURAL RESOURCES

PAMELA FEHL

Ferguson Publishing
An imprint of Infobase Publishing

Green Careers: Environment and Natural Resources

Ferguson
An imprint of Infobase Publishing
132 West 31st Street
New York NY 10001

Library of Congress Cataloging-in-Publication Data
Fehl, Pamela.
    Environment and natural resources / Pamela Fehl. — 1st ed.
        p. cm. — (Green careers)
    Includes bibliographical references and index.
    ISBN-13: 978-0-8160-8151-6 (hardcover : alk. paper)
    ISBN-10: 0-8160-8151-4 (hardcover : alk. paper) 1. Environmentalists—
Vocational guidance—Juvenile literature. 2. Conservationists—Vocational
guidance—Juvenile literature. I. Title.
    GE60.F45 2010
    333.72023—dc22   2009045039

Ferguson books are available at special discounts when purchased in bulk
quantities for businesses, associations, institutions, or sales promotions.
Please call our Special Sales Department in New York at (212) 967-8800 or
(800) 322-8755.

You can find Ferguson on the World Wide Web at http://www.fergpubco.com

Text design by Annie O'Donnell
Composition by EJB Publishing Services
Cover printed by Bang Printing, Brainerd, MN
Book printed and bound by Bang Printing, Brainerd, MN
Date printed: April 2010
Printed in the United States of America

10 9 8 7 6 5 4 3 2 1

This book is printed on acid-free paper.

All links and Web addresses were checked and verified to be correct at the time
of publication. Because of the dynamic nature of the Web, some addresses and
links may have changed since publication and may no longer be valid.

Contents

Introduction

In earlier times, people did not think about the impact of their actions on the environment and on future generations. Mankind hunted certain animals out of existence; damaged or destroyed ecosystems to build industrial plants, buildings, homes, and other developments; polluted the air and waterways; and negatively impacted the health of human beings. The Native American Iroquois Confederacy has a tenet it mandates its chiefs to follow, one to which people today are now paying attention: It simply states that a chief consider how each of his actions will affect his descendants seven generations into the future. If we were to each follow this Seventh Generation tenet, what would the world be like 50, 100, or 300 years from now?

Mankind is making a conscious effort to have a more harmonious relationship with nature, and to be a better steward of the environment. "Conserving," "preserving," and "protecting" have become common buzzwords for sustainable living. People are taking greater interest in the quality of the air they breathe and the water they drink. They are also more concerned about safely treating and disposing of waste, and recycling as much as possible. Organic foods and produce are in greater demand, and in an effort to help support farmers and get fresh foods to urban communities, more farmers' markets are opening every year. Educating and informing the public about land and wildlife conservation efforts and programs, and the ways in which people can get involved, has also become part of everyday life.

The environment and natural resources field offers numerous job titles and opportunities for people with diverse educational backgrounds, skills, and talents. The jobs featured here are merely a small sampling meant to introduce you to some of the specialties within the industry. In this volume, you will find: air quality engineer, arborist, farmers' market manager/promoter, fish and game warden, forester, forestry technician, groundwater professional, naturalist, organic farmer, organic food distributor, range manager, recycling coordinator, soil conservationist and technician, sustainability professional, and wastewater treatment plant operator and technician.

Each profile has 12 sections that help you learn more about different aspects of the job and allow you to determine if your interests and skills match the requirements.

※ **Quick Facts** is a rundown of the basics about the job, including salary range and outlook.

※ **Overview** gives a quick summary, in just a few sentences, about the overall job responsibilities.

※ Some jobs in the environment and natural resources field have been around for a long time, while others are still new and evolving. They all got their start somewhere, though, and the **History** section tells you how and why they began.

※ **The Job** gives you the lowdown on the daily responsibilities. Some profiles also include comments and insights from people working in the field.

※ You can map out the course work you'll need to take by reading the **Requirements** section. It leads you from high school and undergraduate, to postgraduate studies and beyond. **Other Requirements** helps you see if your character traits and skills line up with those needed to enjoy and thrive in the job.

※ The **Exploring** section offers ideas for ways to learn more about the field and the job. You'll find recommendations for books and magazines, professional associations, Web sites, and more.

※ **Employers** focuses on the types of industries and companies that hire the worker that's featured, and may include statistics regarding the number of professionals employed in the United States, and the states and/or cities in which most professionals are concentrated. Statistics are often derived from the U.S. Department of Labor (DoL), the National Association of Colleges and Employers, and professional industry-related associations.

※ **Starting Out** gives you tips on the steps you can start taking now toward learning more about this job and getting your foot in the door.

※ Career paths vary within each job. The **Advancement** section explains a bit about the ways someone can "move up" within the field.

※ You'll find salary ranges for the specific job and related jobs in the **Earnings** section. Information is based on surveys conducted by the DoL, and sometimes from such employment specialists as Salary.com.

※ The **Work Environment** section describes the typical surroundings and conditions of employment—whether indoors or outdoors, noisy or quiet, social or independent.

Also discussed are typical hours worked, any seasonal fluctuations, and the stresses and strains of the job.

* What does the future hold for the job? The **Outlook** section sheds light on whether employment opportunities will abound in the years to come, or if there will be more applicants than positions to fill. Most jobs depend on the economy. When things are looking up, jobs are abundant. When things slow down, fewer jobs exist and competition heats up. The forecast may be based on DoL surveys, professional associations' studies, or experts' insights on the field.

* **For More Information**, at the end of each profile, provides you with listings and contact information for professional associations you may want to join, and other resources you can use to learn more about the job.

Air Quality Engineers

QUICK FACTS

School Subjects
Biology
Chemistry
Mathematics

Personal Skills
Communication/ideas
Technical/scientific

Work Environment
Primarily indoors
Primarily one location

Minimum Education Level
Bachelor's degree

Salary Range
$45,310 to $92,750 to
$115,430+

Certification or Licensing
Required

Outlook
Much faster than the average

OVERVIEW

Air quality engineers, or *air pollution control engineers*, are responsible for developing techniques to analyze and control air pollution by using sophisticated monitoring, chemical analysis, computer modeling, and statistical analysis. Some air quality engineers are involved in pollution-control equipment design or modification. Government-employed air quality experts keep track of a region's polluters, enforce federal regulations, and impose fines or take other action against those who do not comply with regulations. Privately employed engineers may monitor companies' emissions for certain targeted pollutants to ensure that they are within acceptable levels. Air quality engineers who work in research seek ways to combat or avoid air pollution.

HISTORY

The growth of cities and factories during the industrial revolution was a major contributor to the decline of air quality. Some contaminates (pollutants) have always been with us; for instance, particulate matter (tiny solid particles) from very large fires, volcanic eruption, or dust caused by wind. However, human populations were not concentrated enough, nor did the technology exist, to produce conditions that are today considered hazardous until about 200 years ago. The industrialization of England in the 1750s, followed by France in the 1830s and Germany in the 1850s, created high-density populations of millions of people who were drawn to cities to work in the smoke-belching factories, which led to huge increases in airborne pollutants. Work conditions in the factories were notoriously bad, and with no pollution-control or safety measures, living conditions in cities rapidly became equally bad. The severely polluted air was a major cause of respiratory diseases and other illnesses.

America's cities were slightly smaller (and more spread out) and slower to industrialize than Old World capitals like London. Even so, levels of sulfur dioxide were so high in Pittsburgh in the early 1900s that ladies' stockings would disintegrate upon prolonged exposure to the air. The rapid growth of the American automobile industry in the first half of the 20th century contributed greatly to air pollution in two ways: initially, from the steel factories and production plants that made economic giants out of places like Pittsburgh and Detroit, and then from the cars themselves. This became an even greater problem as cars enabled people to move out from the fetid industrial city and commute to work from the suburbs. Mobility independent of public transportation greatly increased auto exhaust and created such modern nightmares as rush-hour traffic.

The effects of air pollution were and are numerous. Particulate matter reacts chemically with heat to form ground-level ozone, or smog. Sulfur and nitrogen oxides form acid rain, which can cause extensive property damage over long periods. Carbon monoxide, the main automobile pollutant, is deadly at a relatively low level of exposure.

Air pollution affects the environment not only in well-publicized phenomena like acid rain and ozone layer destruction, but in less obvious ways as well. For example, increased asthma rates in cities have often been statistically tied to the amount of pollution in the environment. Because pollution is so difficult to remove from the air, and because its effects are so difficult to alter, the problem tends to be cumulative, creating an increasingly critical public health issue.

Some private air pollution control was implemented in the 20th century, mainly to prevent factories from ruining their own works with corrosive and unhealthy emissions. The first attempt at governmental regulation was the Clean Air Act in 1955, but because environmental concerns were not considered viable economic or political issues, this act was not very effective.

As environmentalists became increasingly visible and vigorous campaigners, the Air Quality Act was established in 1967. The Environmental Protection Agency (EPA) created National Ambient Air Quality Standards (NAAQS) in 1971, which set limits on ozone, carbon monoxide, sulfur dioxide, lead, nitrogen dioxide, and particulate levels in the emissions of certain industries and processes. States were supposed to design and implement plans to meet the NAAQS, but so few complied that Congress was forced to extend deadlines three times. Even now, many goals set by the first generation of air-quality regulations remain unmet, and new pollution issues demand attention. Airborne toxins, indoor air pollution, acid rain, carbon dioxide buildup (the greenhouse effect), and depletion of the ozone are now subjects of international controversy and concern.

THE JOB

Several years ago, the EPA composed a list of more than 150 regions of the United States that are out of compliance with federal air quality regulations—some dramatically so—and provided deadlines within the next 20 years to bring these areas under control. The EPA regulations cover everything from car emissions to the greenhouse effect and have the weight of law behind them. There are few industries that will not be touched somehow by this legislation and few that will not require the services of an air quality engineer in the years to come.

Air quality engineers are the professionals who monitor targeted industries or sources to determine whether they are operating within acceptable emissions levels. These engineers suggest changes in the setup of specific companies, or even whole industries, to lessen their impact on the atmosphere. There will be ample opportunity in this field to combine interests because it is a new field with job paths yet to be established. An air quality engineer with some background in meteorology, for example, might track the spread of airborne pollutants through various weather systems by using computer modeling techniques. Another air quality engineer might research indoor air pollution, discovering causes for the "sick building syndrome" and creating new architectural standards and building codes for safe ventilation and construction materials.

Air quality engineers work for the government, in private industry, as consultants, and in research and development. Government

An air quality engineer scrapes soot from playground equipment. The sample will be sent to a lab for testing. *AP Photo/Beaver County Times/Sally Maxson*

employees are responsible for monitoring a region, citing infractions, and otherwise enforcing government regulations. These workers may be called on to give testimony in cases against noncompliant companies. They must deal with public concerns and opinions and are themselves regulated by government bureaucracy and regulations.

Air quality engineers in private industry work for large companies to ensure that air quality regulations are being met. They might be responsible for developing instrumentation to continuously monitor emissions, for example, and using the data to formulate methods of control. They may interact with federal regulators or work independently. Engineers working in private industry also might be involved in what is known as "impact assessment with the goal of sustainable development." This means figuring out the most environmentally sound way to produce products—from raw material to disposal stages—while maintaining or, if possible, increasing the company's profits.

Engineers who work alone as consultants or for consulting firms do many of the same things as engineers in private industry, perhaps for smaller companies that do not need a full-time engineer but still need help meeting federal requirements. They, too, might suggest changes to be implemented by a company to reduce air pollution. Some consultants specialize in certain areas of pollution control. Many private consultants are responsible for selling, installing, and running a particular control system. The job requires some salesmanship and the motivation to maintain a variable clientele.

Finally, engineers committed to research and development may work in public or private research institutions and in academic environments. They may tackle significant problems that affect any number of industries and may improve air quality standards by discovering new contaminates that need regulation.

REQUIREMENTS
High School
High school students should develop their skills in chemistry, math, biology, and ecology.

Postsecondary Training
To break into this field, a bachelor's degree in civil, environmental, or chemical engineering is required. Advancement, specialization, or jobs in research may require a master's degree or Ph.D. Besides

the regular environmental or chemical engineering curricula at the college level, future air quality engineers might engage in some mechanical or civil engineering if they are interested in product development. Modelers and planners should have a good knowledge of computer systems. Supporting course work in biology, toxicology, or meteorology can give the job seeker an edge for certain specialized positions even before gaining experience in the workforce.

Certification or Licensing

All engineers who do work that affects public health, safety, or property must register with the state. To obtain registration, engineers must have a degree from an accredited engineering program. Right before they get their degree (or soon after), they must pass an engineer-in-training (EIT) exam covering fundamentals of science and engineering. A few years into their careers, engineers also must pass an exam covering engineering practices.

Other Requirements

Prospective air quality engineers should be puzzle solvers. The ability to work with intangibles is a trait of successful air quality management. As in most fields, communications skills are vital. Engineers must be able to clearly communicate their ideas and findings, both orally and in writing, to a variety of people with different levels of technical understanding.

EXPLORING

You can begin investigating air quality engineering by reading environmental science and engineering periodicals, which are available in many large libraries. Familiarizing yourself with the current issues involving air pollution will give you a better idea of what problems will be facing this field in the near future.

The next step might be a call to a local branch of the EPA. In addition to providing information about local source problems, they can also provide a breakdown of air quality standards that must be met and who has to meet them.

To get a better idea about college-level course work and possible career directions, contact major universities, environmental associations, or even private environmental firms. Some private consulting firms will explain how specific areas of study combine to create their particular area of expertise.

Good Ozone, Bad Ozone

Stratospheric ozone is located in the stratosphere, the layer of the earth's atmosphere that is between eight and 30 miles above the earth's surface. This layer of the atmosphere is too far away for us to breathe, thus the ozone contained in it is not harmful to us. Rather, it actually protects plants and animals from the sun's harmful ultraviolet rays. Thus, stratospheric ozone is the "good ozone."

Tropospheric ozone, or "bad ozone," is located in the troposphere, the layer of the earth's atmosphere running from the ground to eight miles above it. This is the air that we *do* breathe. Ozone does not naturally occur in the troposphere. It forms there as a result of a combination of emissions from automobiles, factories, and certain household products that get trapped in the troposphere. On hot and humid days in certain parts of the country (in big cities, especially), tropospheric ozone levels can become quite high, making breathing difficult for many people.

An easy way to remember the difference between good and bad ozone in relation to the earth's atmosphere is "Good up high, bad nearby."

Source: Environmental Protection Agency

EMPLOYERS

In 2006 there were about 54,000 environmental engineers employed in the United States, according to the U.S. Department of Labor. Most air quality engineers are privately employed in industries subject to emissions control, such as manufacturing. They may also work for the federal government, investigating and ensuring compliance with air quality regulations, as consultants to private industry and large companies, and in research and development. They may also work at universities that teach and conduct research on air-quality and environmental control, and for private and government laboratories that develop new generations of pollution-control systems

STARTING OUT

Summer positions as an air pollution technician provide valuable insight into the engineer's job as well as contacts and experience. Check with local and state EPA offices and larger consulting firms in your area for internship positions and their requirements. Environmentally oriented engineers may be able to volunteer for citizen watchdog group monitoring programs, patrolling regions for previously undiscovered or unregulated contaminates. Most air quality engineers can expect to get jobs in their field immediately after graduating with a bachelor's degree. Your school career services office can assist you in fine-tuning your resume and setting up interviews with potential employers. Government positions are a common point of entry; high turnover rates open positions as experienced engineers leave for the more lucrative private sector, which accounts for four out of five jobs in air quality management. An entry-level job might focus on monitoring and analysis.

ADVANCEMENT

With experience and education, the engineer might develop a specialization within the field of air quality. Research grants are sometimes available to experienced engineers who wish to concentrate on specific problems or areas of study. Management is another avenue of advancement. The demand for technically oriented middle management in the private sector makes engineers with good interpersonal skills very valuable.

In many ways, advancement will be dictated by the increasing value of air quality engineers to business and industry in general. Successful development of air-pollution control equipment or systems—perhaps that even cut costs as they reduce pollution—will make air quality engineers important players in companies' economic strategies. As regulations tighten and increasing emphasis is put on minimizing environmental impact, air quality engineers will be in the spotlight as both regulators and innovators. Advancement may come in the form of monetary incentives, bonuses, or management positions.

EARNINGS

According to the Department of Labor, the lowest paid 10 percent of environmental scientists earned about $45,310 per year in 2008. The middle 50 percent earned between $56,980 and $94,280; the top paid 10 percent earned more than $115,430. The median federal government salary (among the highest in the industry) was $92,750. Fringe benefits may include tuition reimbursement programs, use of a company vehicle for fieldwork, full health coverage, and retirement plans.

WORK ENVIRONMENT

Working conditions differ depending on the employer, the specialization of the position, and the location of the job. An air quality engineer may be required to perform fieldwork, such as observing emission sources, but more often works in an office, determining the factors responsible for airborne pollutants and devising ways to prevent them. Coworkers may include other environmental engineers, lab technicians, and office personnel. An engineer may discuss specific problems with a company's economic planners and develop programs to make that company more competitive environmentally and economically. Those who monitor emissions have considerable responsibility and therefore considerable pressure to do their job well—failure to maintain industry standards could cost their employer government fines. Engineers in some consulting firms may be required to help sell the system they develop or work with.

Most engineers work a standard 40-hour week, putting in overtime to solve critical problems as quickly as possible. A large part of the job for most air quality engineers consists of keeping up to date with federal regulations, industry and regional standards, and developments in their area of expertise. Some employers require standard business attire, while some require more fieldwork from their engineers and thus may not enforce rigorous dress codes. Unlike water and soil pollution, air pollution can sometimes be difficult to measure quantitatively if the source is unknown. Major pollutants are generally easily identified (although not so easily eliminated), but traces of small "leaks" may literally change with the wind and make for time-consuming, deliberate, and frustrating work.

OUTLOOK

Job growth for air quality engineers should be much faster than the average for all occupations through 2016, according to the U.S. Department of Labor. When the immediate scramble to modify and monitor equipment slackens as government regulations are met in the next 20 years, the focus in air quality engineering will shift from traditional "end of pipe" controls (e.g., modifying catalytic converters or gasoline to make cars burn gas more cleanly) to source control (developing alternative fuels and eliminating oil-based industrial emissions). As mentioned, impact assessment will play a large part on the corporate side of air quality management, as businesses strive to stay profitable in the wake of public health and safety regulations. Air pollution problems like greenhouse gas buildup and ozone pollution will not disappear in the near future and will be increasingly vital areas of research. International development will allow American pollution control engineers to offer their services in any part of the world that has growing industries or populations. Pollution control in general has a big future, and air pollution control is quickly taking up a major chunk of the expected expenditures and revenues in this category.

FOR MORE INFORMATION

For information on student chapters, scholarships, and a list of colleges and degrees offering environmental degrees, contact

Air and Waste Management Association
420 Fort Duquesne Boulevard
One Gateway Center, 3rd Floor
Pittsburgh, PA 15222-1435
Tel: 800-270-3444
Email: info@awma.org
http://www.awma.org

To find state and local air agencies and learn more about air pollution and initiatives, visit

National Association of Clean Air Agencies
444 North Capitol Street, NW, Suite 307
Washington, DC 20001-1506
Tel: 202-624-7864
http://www.cleanairworld.org

For general information about air quality and other environmental issues, contact

U.S. Environmental Protection Agency
Ariel Rios Building
1200 Pennsylvania Avenue, NW
Washington, DC 20004-2403
Tel: 202-272-0167
http://www.epa.gov

Arborists

OVERVIEW

Arborists are professionals who practice arboriculture, which is the care of trees and shrubs, especially those found in urban areas. Arborists prune and fertilize trees and other woody plants as well as monitor them for insects and diseases. Arborists are often consulted for various tree-related issues.

HISTORY

Arboriculture developed as a branch of the plant science of horticulture. While related to the study of forestry, arborists view their specimens on an individual level; foresters manage trees as a group.

Trees are important to the environment. Besides releasing oxygen back to the atmosphere, trees enrich the soil with their fallen, decaying leaves, and their roots aid in the prevention of soil erosion. Trees provide shelter and a source of food for many different types of animals. People use trees as ornamentation. Trees are often planted to protect against the wind and glare of the sun, block offensive views, mark property lines, and provide privacy. Green architects and builders also factor existing trees into their designs of homes and buildings, to help cool the interiors naturally and save on energy costs. Trees and shrubs often add considerably to a home's property value.

All trees need proper care and seasonal maintenance. The occupation of *tree surgeon*, as arborists were first known, came from the need for qualified individuals to care for trees and shrubs, as well as woody vines and ground-cover plants. Trees planted in busy city areas and in the suburbs face pollution, traffic, crowding, extreme temperatures, and other daily hazards. City trees often have a large percentage of their roots covered with concrete. Roots of larger trees sometimes interfere with plumbing pipes, sidewalks, and building foundations. Branches can interfere with buildings or power lines. Trees located along the sides of roads and highways must be maintained; branches are pruned, and fallen leaves and fruit are gathered. Proper intervention, if not prevention, of diseases is an important task of arborists.

THE JOB

Trees and shrubs need more than just sunlight and water. That's where arborists take over. Arborists, who may also be known as *tree trimmers and pruners*, as well as *landscaping and groundskeeping workers*, perform many different tasks for trees and shrubs, some for the sake of maintenance and others for the tree's health and well-being.

Pruning. All trees need some amount of pruning to control their shape; sometimes limbs are trimmed if they interfere with power lines, if they cross property lines, or if they grow too close to houses and other buildings. Arborists may use tools such as pruning shears or hand and power saws to do the actual cutting. If the branches are especially large or cumbersome, arborists may rope them together before the sawing begins. After cutting, the branches can be safely lowered to the ground. Ladders, aerial lifts, and cranes may be used to reach extremely tall trees. Sometimes arborists need to cable or brace tree limbs weakened by disease or old age or damaged by a storm.

Planting or transplanting. When cities or towns plan a new development, or wish to gentrify an existing one, they often consult with arborists to determine what types of trees to plant. Arborists can suggest trees that will thrive in a certain environment. Young plantings, or immature trees, are more cost effective and are often used, though sometimes larger, more mature trees are transplanted to the desired location.

An arborist measures a tree estimated to be 350 years old. *AP Photo/Knoxville News-Sentinel, Joe Howell*

Diagnosis and treatment. A large part of keeping a tree healthy is the prevention of disease. There are a number of diseases that affect trees, among them anthracnose and Dutch elm disease. Insects such as the Asian longhorned beetle and the dogwood borer, to name only a few, pose a potential threat to trees, and have done considerable damage to certain species in the past, by boring into the trunk or spreading disease-causing organisms. Bacteria, fungi, viruses, and disease-causing organisms can also be fatal enemies of trees. Arborists are specially trained to identify the insect or the disease weakening the tree and apply the necessary remedy or medication. Common methods prescribed by arborists include chemical insecticides, or the use of natural insect predators to combat the problem. Arborists closely monitor insect migrations or any other situations that may be harmful to a species of tree.

When a tree is too old or badly diseased, arborists may choose to cut it down. Arborists will carefully cut the tree into pieces to prevent injury to people or damage to surrounding property.

Prevention. Trees, especially young plantings, often need extra nourishment. Arborists are trained to apply fertilizers, both natural and chemical, in a safe and environmentally friendly manner. Golf courses and parks also hire arborists to install lightning-protection systems for lone trees or mature, valuable trees.

REQUIREMENTS
High School
High school biology classes can provide you with a solid background to be a successful arborist. An interest in gardening, conservation, or the outdoors is also helpful.

Postsecondary Training
Take classes in botany, chemistry, horticulture, and plant pathology. Several colleges and universities offer programs in arboriculture and other related fields such as landscape design, nursery stock production, or grounds and turf maintenance. Entry-level positions such as assistants or climbers do not need a college degree for employment. Advanced education, however, is highly desired if you plan to make this field your career.

Certification or Licensing
The Tree Care Industry Association (TCIA) and the International Society of Arboriculture (ISA) both offer various home-study courses and books on arboriculture. Most arborists are certified or licensed. Licensure ensures an arborist meets the state's regulations for working with pesticides and herbicides. Check with your local government—not all states require arborists to be licensed. Certification, given by the ISA after completion of required training and education, is considered by many as a measure of an arborist's skill and experience in the industry. Today's savvy consumers look for certified arborists when it comes to caring for their trees and other precious landscaping plants. Arborists need to apply for recertification every three years and must complete 30 units of continuing education classes and seminars.

EXPLORING
Learn more about tree care and the industry by visiting Web sites such as ISA (http://www.isa-arbor.com) and TCIA (http://128.241.193.252/index.aspx). If you really want to test

the waters, see if you can find part-time or summer work with an arborist. You'll earn extra spending money while also learning firsthand about the industry. Check with the TCIA for a complete listing of certified arborists in your area.

EMPLOYERS

Landscaping companies and businesses that offer a host of expert tree services are common employers of arborists. Employment opportunities are also available with municipal governments, botanical gardens, and arboretums. For example, an arborist in the Chicago area may want to seek a position with the Chicago Botanic Gardens or the Morton Arboretum; both places are known for their lush gardens and wooded trails. According to the Department of Labor, there were about 1.2 million landscaping and groundskeeping workers, and 41,000 tree trimmers and pruners, employed in the United States in 2006.

STARTING OUT

So you've decided to become an arborist—what's the next step? Start by compiling a list of tree-care firms in your area, then see if they have Web sites that list job openings. You can either reply online or get contact information and call or email them directly. Another great option is working with the highway or parks department of your city or county—they often hire crews to maintain their trees.

Many colleges and universities offer job placement services or post employment opportunities on their Web site and in their career services office. Industry associations and trade magazines are also good sources of job openings.

Don't plan to climb to the top of an American elm your first day on the job. Expect to stay at ground level for at least several months. Trainees in this industry start as *helpers* or *ground workers*, who load and unload equipment from trucks, gather branches and other debris for disposal, handle ropes, and give assistance to climbers. They also operate the chipper—a machine that cuts large branches into small chips. After some time observing more experienced workers, trainees are allowed to climb smaller trees or the lower limbs of large trees. They are also taught the proper way to operate large machinery and climbing gear. Most companies provide on-the-job training that lasts from one to three months.

ADVANCEMENT

Experienced arborists can advance to supervisory positions such as crew manager or department supervisor. Another option is to become a consultant in the field and work for tree care firms, city or town boards, large nurseries, or gardening groups.

Arborists with a strong entrepreneurial nature can choose to open their own business, but aspiring entrepreneurs must make sure that their business skills are up to par. Even the most talented and hard-working arborists won't stand a chance if they can't balance their accounts or market their services properly.

Advancement to other industries related to arboriculture is another possibility. Some arborists choose to work in landscape design, forestry, or other fields of horticulture.

EARNINGS

The U.S. Department of Labor lists the median yearly salary of tree trimmers and pruners as $29,970 in 2008. The bottom 10 percent earned $20,000 a year or less, and the top 10 percent earned $46,480 a year or more.

Salaries vary greatly depending on many factors, among them the size and location of the company and the experience of the arborist. Arborists servicing busy urban areas tend to earn more. In 2008 the median annual income for tree trimmers and pruners who worked for buildings and dwellings was $30,260, while those working for the federal government brought home $48,340 per year. The top-paying states were Connecticut, Delaware, Hawaii, New York, and Washington.

Full-time employees receive a benefits package including health insurance, life insurance, paid vacation and sick time, and paid holidays. Most tree companies supply necessary uniforms, tools, equipment, and training.

WORK ENVIRONMENT

Much of an arborist's work is physically demanding, and most of it is done outdoors. Arborists work throughout the year, though their busiest times are the spring and summer. Tasks done at this time include fertilizing, pruning, and prevention spraying. During the winter months, arborists can expect to care for trees injured or damaged by excess snow, ice storms, or floods.

Equipment such as sharp saws, grinders, chippers, bulldozers, tractors, and other large machinery can be potentially dangerous for arborists. There is also the risk of falling from the top of a tall tree, many of which reach heights of 50 feet or more. Arborists rely on cleated shoes, security belts, and safety hoists to make their job easier as well as safer.

OUTLOOK

The future of arboriculture looks promising. The U.S Department of Labor predicts faster than average growth for this field through 2016. The public's increasing interest in the preservation of the environment has increased demand for qualified arborists. Many homeowners are willing to pay top dollar for professionally designed and maintained landscaping. Increased resistance to pesticides and new species of insects pose constant threats to all trees. While travel abroad is easier and, in a sense, has made the world smaller, it has also placed the environment at risk. For example, Asian long-horned beetles were unknowingly transported to the United States via packing material. By the time the insects were discovered in 1996, the beetles had irreversibly damaged hundreds of mature trees throughout New York, Chicago, and surrounding areas. These beetles have no known predator and their path of tree destruction continues to this day. Arborists, especially those trained to diagnose and treat such cases, will be in demand to work in urban areas.

FOR MORE INFORMATION

From tree identification to caring for our fine-leafed friends, everything you want to know about trees can be found here.
Arbor Day Foundation
100 Arbor Avenue
Nebraska City, NE 68410-1067
Tel: 888-448-7337
http://www.arborday.org/generalinfo/

For industry and career information, or to receive a copy of Arborist News *or* Careers in Arboriculture, *contact*
International Society of Arboriculture
PO 3129
Champaign, IL 61826-3129

Tel: 217-355-9411
Email: isa@isa-arbor.com
http://www.isa-arbor.com

For industry and career information, a listing of practicing arborists, or educational programs at the university level, or home study, contact
Tree Care Industry Association
136 Harvey Road, Suite 101
Londonderry, NH 03053-7439
Tel: 800-733-2622
Email: membership@tcia.org
http://128.241.193.252/index.aspx

Farmers' Market Managers/Promoters

QUICK FACTS

School Subjects
Business
Earth science
English
Math

Personal Skills
Business/management
Communication/ideas

Work Environment
Indoors and outdoors
One or more locations

Minimum Education Level
Bachelor's degree

Salary Range
$8,864 to $21,912
to $61,970

Certification or Licensing
Required in some states

Outlook
About as fast as the
average

OVERVIEW

Farmers' market managers/promoters manage farmers' markets, ensuring that operations comply with laws and regulations. Their duties are diverse, ranging from enlisting farmers to participate in the market and promoting the market to consumers, to hiring and managing staff, scheduling events, and handling correspondence and record and bookkeeping. They may work for one market or multiple markets within specific regions.

HISTORY

Farmers' markets provide opportunities for farmers and craftsmen to sell their products—fruits, vegetables, herbs, cheeses, meats, baked goods, etc.—directly to consumers. They date back to ancient times, when public markets were the few places in existence where residents could find the items they needed for daily living. Cities encouraged public markets as a way to bring local and regional producers to the city to increase their business, as well as a way to help residents get healthy food that was priced fairly. Public markets also provided employment opportunities, encouraged farming near the city, and, as a result, helped prevent people from moving away.

One early American public market was the city-owned High Street Market in Philadelphia. The market started with just a few stalls in the early 1800s, and by the 1850s had grown to a series of sheds stretching across many streets, with breaks only at the intersections. Market space was organized and divided according to the types of products being sold, such as vegetables, herbs, roots, produce, meat, fish, and earthenware. High Street Market was torn down in 1859 to make way for the construction of large, market houses that were owned by private companies. This followed the movement away from municipally owned and operated farmers' markets of the previous decades and toward privatization of the business. Today most farmers' markets operate on public property, with sponsorship from such nongovernmental groups as farmers' associations, chambers of commerce, community organizations, or food cooperatives.

Farmers' markets are set up in various ways to fit in with their environment. Some use already existing structures, such as bridges and elevated highways, as cover. For others, where these types of structures are not available, stalls are built, and tarps and other materials are used for shelter. Many markets are open year-round, rain or shine, with limited days and hours of operation each week. They sell what is being grown that season.

Farmer's markets may be temporary setups (easy to assemble and break down), situated in open squares in cities, such as the Union Square Greenmarket in New York City. The Council on the Environment of New York City started this market, and others like it, in 1976, after years of city residents complaining bitterly about the "brown lettuce" and "hard tomatoes" that were being sold in supermarkets. The first greenmarket in New York City consisted of 12 farmers in an empty lot, and has grown since to become a large network of greenmarkets throughout the five boroughs.

Pike Place Market in Seattle, Washington, is an example of an older, well-established public market situated in a permanent structure. The origins of the nine-acre, 102-year-old Pike Place Market are symbolic of the spirit that still drives many farmers' markets today. The price of onions had increased tenfold between 1906 and 1907, and citizens were outraged and were not going to take it any longer. Middlemen had been gouging prices for years and people were tired of being ripped off. Seattle City Councilman Thomas Reveille came up with the idea of a public street market, where farmers could sell directly to consumers, therefore eliminating the middleman. Pike Place Market "opened" on August 17, 1907, with eight farmers selling produce from their wagons at the corner of Pike Street and First Avenue. Approximately 10,000 shoppers showed up, and by 11:00 A.M., the wagons were sold out of produce. The Pike Market building opened at the end of 1907. Today, the market features 200 year-round commercial businesses; 190 craftspeople; and 120 farmers who rent table space by the day.

Consumer demand for locally grown, fresh food continues to grow, and more farmers' markets are starting up every year. Between 1994 and 2008, the number of farmers' markets operating in the United States had risen from 1,788 to 4,685.

THE JOB

Farmers' market managers/promoters oversee markets in which farmers sell their products to consumers. Because farming is seasonal, more than two-thirds of all managers work for markets that are set up in temporary facilities. According to a 2006 survey conducted by the Agricultural Marketing Service of the U.S. Department of Agriculture (USDA), farmers' markets in 2005 averaged 48,857 square feet in size, which is about the size of a medium-sized retail grocery store. The smallest farmers' market was 20 square feet, and the largest was 3.4 million square feet.

As with most management positions in other industries, farmers' market managers are responsible for a variety of tasks. The vending stalls need to be filled with farmers, so managers work closely with farmers, meeting with them to promote the market, field their questions, and negotiate the terms for vending. They set up contracts, vending sites, and schedules. They are also responsible for hiring staff and volunteers, and managing and overseeing their work. Another big part of the job is customer relations. Many management positions require previous experience in handling customers. This means not only addressing questions and concerns while on-site at the market, but responding to consumers' emails and phone calls when working in the office.

The Pacific Coast Farmers' Market Association described the job requirements for a market manager as follows: making sure the market operates in compliance with state law, health regulations, and association rules and regulations; overseeing the set-up, operation, cleanliness, and shutdown of the market; collecting payment from

FARMER'S MARKET TERMS

Certified Farmers' Market Some states, such as California, Nevada, and Texas, require farmers' markets to be certified, to ensure that farmers have, in fact, produced the products that are being sold.

EBT Electronic Benefits Transfer, an electronic system that allows SNAP (Supplemental Nutritional Assistance Program) participants to buy fresh foods by transferring their government benefits to a retailer account. Many farmers' markets are technologically equipped to accept SNAP benefits.

SFMNP The Senior Farmers' Market Nutrition Program, in which eligible low-income seniors can exchange coupons for fresh fruits, vegetables, honey, and herbs at farmers' markets.

WIC FMNP The Women, Infants, and Children Farmers' Market Nutrition Program provides coupons for fresh food to eligible low-income women who are pregnant or caring for children up to five years old who are at nutritional risk.

Source: Farmers' Market Coalition

farmers at the end of each market day; updating business logs and reports, and making bank deposits; setting up and running a market information booth to address customers' questions; and assisting in scheduling and hosting farmers' market events.

A farmers' market manager/promoter is also responsible for advertising and marketing the market to attract consumers. He or she may create the ads and flyers, or hire an artist or graphic designer to create promotions for newspapers and magazines, as well as a Web designer to work on the market's Web site. The manager/promoter also spreads word about the market by networking and building relationships with businesses located within the community where the farmers' market is located.

REQUIREMENTS
High School
If you are interested in this work, a well-rounded high school education should include course work in business, math, earth science,

English, and computers. Take classes in agriculture and ecology if your school offers them. Knowledge of another language can be beneficial in communicating with customers, employees, and farmers from other countries, so be sure to take foreign language classes as well.

Postsecondary Training

Some farmers' markets may require managers to have an undergraduate degree, while others may prefer prior work experience at a farmers' market. Course work in business, marketing, advertising, agriculture, social sciences, environmental studies, communications, and English are beneficial.

Certification or Licensing

Some states, such as California, Nevada, and Texas, require that farmers' markets be certified to ensure that farmers have produced the products being sold. Contact your state's market representatives for more information

Other Requirements

Management positions, in general, require strong, clear communication skills. This is especially true for farmers' market managers. They deal with a wide range of people, from the general public to farmers and employees. Patience, flexibility, and diplomacy serve this type of work well. Knowledge of farming and farming products is also especially helpful. Familiarity with software programs, such as MS Word, Excel, and Publisher are essential for administrative work. And fluency in another language, such as Spanish, may come in handy. Creative skills are useful in successfully advertising and promoting farmers' markets. Negotiation skills are also helpful in attracting and securing vendors for the market.

EXPLORING

The best way to learn more about the farmers' market management field is to talk to a manager directly. You can find a market near you by visiting the USDA's National Directory of Farmers' Markets (http://apps.ams.usda.gov/FarmersMarkets/) and keying in your zip code. Most farmers' markets have their own Web sites, so be sure to browse through them and find the hours of operation. When you visit the market, be sure to talk with farmers and market employees. Ask them what their work entails, what's involved in participating in the farmers' market, and if the market manager is onsite and available to chat. Trade publications and books about the farmers' market business will give you further insight and understanding of the various facets of this type of work. The bi-monthly trade publication *Farmers' Markets Today* (http://www.farmersmarketstoday.com) provides useful information for farmers' market managers, vendors, and farmers. You can also find numerous books targeted at farmers' marketing by visiting the Books for Farmers' Markets Web site (http://www.farmersmarketonline.com/a/farmersmarketbooks.htm).

EMPLOYERS

As you may have guessed, farmers' market managers and promoters work for farmers' markets. They may work for a single-business operation, and therefore be located at just one site, or they may be responsible for several farmers' markets or more within one or more counties.

STARTING OUT

Volunteering or working part time at a farmers' market is the best way to see firsthand how a market operates and what managers deal with on a regular basis. Membership in a professional association for farmers' market managers also provides access to educational workshops, events and conferences, networking opportunities, and job listings. You can find such resources by visiting the Web site of the National American Farmers' Direct Marketing Association (http://www.nafdma.com), or by conducting an Internet search for a professional association in the state in which you live.

You can also learn a great deal about farmers' markets and see if this work interests you by reading the University of California's Farmers' Market Management Series publications, which are published through the school's Small Farm Program. Titles include *Starting a New Farmers' Market, Management Skills for Marketers,* and *Growing Your Farmers' Market.* Visit http://www.sfc.ucdavis.edu/farmers_market/ for more information.

ADVANCEMENT

Moving up in the farmers' market management field depends on the managers' years of experience. Those who work for small, single-market operations can advance by covering more markets within several counties or regions. Other ways to advance include starting their own farmers' market and consulting with other markets about business and promotion. They might become educators, working for universities that have farmers' market programs. They might also work for nonprofit organizations or government agencies that focus on farming and farmers' markets.

EARNINGS

Salaries for farmers' market managers will vary depending upon the size of the market and the scope of the manager's job. Smaller-sized farmers' markets and those that are relatively young are more dependent upon outside funding than are larger, more established businesses. Farmers' markets that have been around for a long time are usually self-sufficient, able to continue operating based on ven-dors' fees alone. Newer businesses are usually funded by a combina-tion of sources, including vendors' fees, city or county governments, and nonprofit organizations. Many farmers' markets also participate in government-funded nutrition programs as a way to help fund their businesses as well as to help people in need receive better and fresher food. Managers who work for smaller and newer markets tend to have lower salaries, as may be expected. Those who work for larger, older businesses will generally bring in higher annual incomes. Also, because the work is seasonal, managers may be paid on an hourly basis, and may have to seek alternate work when the season ends.

According to findings from a 2006 survey by the USDA Agricul-tural Marketing Service, the average annual salary for paid farmers' market managers in 2005 was $14,323, with the lowest salary at $8,864 in the Rocky Mountain region, and the highest salary at $21,912 in the Mid-Atlantic region.

The U.S. Department of Labor does not cite salaries specific to farmers' market managers, but lists the annual income for supervisors or managers of retail sales workers in 2008 as ranging from $22,210 to $61,970 or more per year. Those who worked for grocery stores averaged $37,390 per year. Farmers' market managers who work in regions where the climate allows for more permanent, year-round marketing may have salaries within these ranges.

WORK ENVIRONMENT

Farmers' markets are usually outdoors in cities, suburbs, and coun-tryside settings. Farmers' market managers/promoters will work at least 40-hour workweeks, which can include weekends. They work indoors in offices, as well as on-site at the markets and in various weather conditions. They may travel to different sites if they manage more than one market, so a valid driver's license and the ability and willingness to drive will be required.

OUTLOOK

Demand for farm-fresh food has been on the rise for more than a decade. To meet this demand, the farmers' market business is also growing, which is good news for farmers' market managers. According to the Agricultural Marketing Service of the U.S. Department of Agriculture, there were 1,755 farmers' markets operating in the United States in 1994. In 2004 that number had more than doubled to 3,706. Since then, even more markets have opened and begun operations. In mid-2008 approximately 4,685 farmers' markets were listed in the National Directory of Farmers' Markets.

While the U.S. Department of Labor forecasts a slight decline in employment opportunities for farmers overall through 2016, many small-scale farming businesses and those in related professions are finding success in specialty niches, such as organic food production as well as in farmers' markets that cater to urban and suburban customers. Farmers' market managers will, therefore, be needed to help build and maintain relationships with farmers and to get word out to consumers about the markets.

FOR MORE INFORMATION

Find farmers' market news, reports, and publications on the American Farmland Trust's Web site.

American Farmland Trust
1200 18th Street, NW, Suite 800
Washington, D.C. 20036-2524
Tel: 202-331-7300
Email: info@farmland.org
http://www.farmland.org

Learn more about agricultural policy and advocacy by visiting FMC's Web site.

Farmers Market Coalition (FMC)
PO Box 4089
Martinsburg, WV 25402-4089
http://www.farmersmarketcoalition.org

To find out more about the Farmers' Market Managers Mentoring Program, contact

Farmers Market Federation of New York
117 Highbridge Street, Suite U-3
Fayetteville, NY 13066-1951
Tel: 315-637-4690
http://www.nyfarmersmarket.com/

Visit this association's Web site for membership information and other resources.

North American Farmers' Direct Marketing Association
62 White Loaf Road
Southampton, MA 01073-9251
Tel: 413-529-0386
http://www.nafdma.com

Learn more about issues regarding food, farming, natural resources, and rural development by visiting

United States Department of Agriculture
  Economic Research Service
1800 M Street, NW
Washington, DC 20036-5831
http://www.ers.usda.gov

Fish and Game Wardens

OVERVIEW

Professional wildlife conservationists, once widely known as *fish and game wardens*, are now known by a variety of titles. Jobs falling under this category in the federal government include *U.S. Fish and Wildlife Service special agents, federal law enforcement officers, wildlife inspectors, refuge rangers*, and *refuge officers*. On a state or municipal level, the job title might be *conservation police, environmental conservation police*, or *conservation wardens*. Along with the job title, the job itself has expanded. Once, fish and game wardens were hired solely to protect wildlife. Today, in addition to that original purpose, they perform a wide variety of tasks related to resource management, public information, and law enforcement. The U.S. Fish and Wildlife Service employs more than 7,500 people.

HISTORY

For centuries wildlife has suffered because of the actions of human beings. Increasingly efficient weaponry—bows, rifles, shotguns— made it easier for people to kill game. ("Game" may be broadly defined as any fish, birds, or mammals that are hunted noncommercially for food, sport, or both.) Some species of animals have been hunted to extinction. Forests have been cleared, swamps drained, and rivers dammed to clear the way for agriculture and industry. These activities have harmed or destroyed large areas of plant and wildlife habitat.

Beginning in the late 19th century, growing concern for vanishing wildlife led to the initiation of comprehensive conservation actions. The governments of the United States and other nations have since passed protective laws and set aside national parks and other reserves for wildlife. The principal agency assigned to the conservation and enhancement of animals and their habitats in this country is the U.S. Fish and Wildlife Service. An agency of the U.S. Department of the Interior, it is responsible for the scientific development of commercial fisheries and the conservation of fish and wildlife. The service, which was officially created in 1940 and with roots dating back to 1871, manages the 93 million-acre National Wildlife Refuge System. This system includes more than 520 National Wildlife Refuges, thousands of smaller wetlands, and other special management areas. It also operates 69 National Fish Hatcheries, 64 fishery resource offices, nine Fish Health Centers, seven Fish Technology Centers, and 78 ecological services field stations.

THE JOB

The conservation of fish and wildlife is a responsibility that grows more complex each year, especially with growing pollution and environmental changes and tighter regulations and laws. To accomplish its mission, the U.S. Fish and Wildlife Service, for example, employs many of the country's best biologists, wildlife managers, engineers, realty specialists, law enforcement agents, and others who work to save endangered and threatened species; conserve migratory birds and inland fisheries; provide expert advice to other federal agencies, industry, and foreign governments; and manage nearly 700 offices and field stations. These personnel work in every state and territory from the Arctic Ocean to the South Pacific, and from the Atlantic to the Caribbean.

Wildlife inspectors and *special agents* are two job titles that have arisen from "fish and game wardens." Wildlife inspectors monitor the legal trade and intercept illegal importations and exportations of federally protected fish and wildlife. At points of entry into the United States, wildlife inspectors examine shipping containers, live animals,

An Oklahoma game warden uses binoculars to survey a lake for violations of hunting and fishing laws. *AP Photo/The Oklahoman/Paul Hellstern*

wildlife products such as animal skins, and documents. Inspectors, who work closely with special agents, may seize shipments as evidence, conduct investigations, and testify in courts of law.

Special agents of the U.S. Fish and Wildlife Service are trained criminal investigators who enforce federal wildlife laws throughout this country. They are highly trained professionals who are statutorily authorized to carry firearms, serve warrants, and make arrests. Special agents conduct law enforcement investigations, which may include activities such as surveillance, undercover work, and preparing cases for court. They often work with other federal, tribal, foreign, state, or local law enforcement authorities. These agents enforce traditional migratory bird regulations and investigate commercial activities involving illegal trade in protected wildlife. Some agents work at border ports to enforce federal laws protecting wildlife that enters into interstate and national commerce.

Another prominent position within the Fish and Wildlife Service is that of a *refuge ranger* or *refuge manager.* These professionals work at more than 520 national refuges across the country, protecting and conserving migratory and native species of birds, mammals, fish, endangered species, and other wildlife. Many of these refuges also offer outdoor recreational opportunities and programs to educate the public about the refuges' wildlife and their habitats.

Beth Ullenberg, Supervisory Visitor Services Manager of the Minnesota Valley National Wildlife Refuge (NWR) in Bloomington, Minnesota, points out that, "Fish and Game Wardens (often called Park Rangers) are law enforcement officers who are now referred to as Conservation Officers. These folks go through a law-enforcement training academy, carry firearms, and can write tickets. In general, Park Rangers can be educators, interpreters, recreational specialists, tour guides, etc." She explains that her position does not include law enforcement authority.

Ullenberg has worked for the U.S. Fish and Wildlife Service for over 16 years. She started her career right out of college, and had worked on national wildlife refuges in Oregon and South Dakota before coming to the Minnesota Valley NWR. As Supervisory Visitor Services Manager, her job involves managing a staff of park rangers who "provide the public with natural resources education, public interpretive programs, hunting and fishing opportunities, wildlife observation and nature photography, and help planning special events, all on the refuge." What she enjoys most about the work is the diversity and the ability to get outdoors. One moment she may be "teaching school kids about wildlife, or staffing [the]

Visitor Center," while the next moment may see her "creating a new hiking trail or even banding ducks!"

The U.S Fish and Wildlife Service also employs people in a wide variety of specialties, such as engineering, ecology, zoology, veterinary science, forestry, botany, chemistry, hydrology, land surveying, architecture, landscape architecture, statistics, library science, archaeology, education, and guidance counseling. The service hires administrators and business managers, realty specialists, appraisers, assessors, contract specialists, purchasing agents, budget analysts, financial managers, computer specialists and programmers, human resources professionals, and public affairs specialists. Additionally, a variety of technical, clerical, and trades and crafts positions are available.

REQUIREMENTS
High School
Take courses in biology and other science subjects, geography, mathematics, social studies, and physical education. See if your high school offers cooperative programs, which will allow you to study as well as work in programs at refuges and other facilities—and in some cases, get paid for some of the hours you work at the facility.

Postsecondary Training
All positions in this category require a bachelor's degree or three years of work-related experience. Higher positions require at least one year of graduate studies; as you move up the scale to increasingly professional positions, master's or even doctoral degrees become mandatory.

Specialized positions require advanced education or training. For example, all biology-related positions require a bachelor's degree in biology or natural-resources management, or a combination of education and experience equivalent to a degree that includes an appropriate number of semester hours in biological science. Visit http://www.fws.gov/jobs/ for an overview of educational requirements for various positions in the service.

Additional on-the-job training is given for most positions. Natural-resource managers and related professionals receive training at the National Conservation Training Center in Shepherdstown, West Virginia. Special agents are given 18 weeks of formal training in criminal investigative and wildlife law enforcement techniques at the Federal Law Enforcement Training Center in Glynco, Georgia.

In addition, the service typically requires its employees to receive 40 hours of training each year.

Other Requirements

Some positions have physical fitness and ability requirements, so you must undergo a battery of physical tests. To qualify for a special agent position, you must meet strict medical, physical, and psychological requirements. You must also participate in mandatory drug testing and psychological screening programs.

Only the most highly qualified candidates will be interviewed for special agent positions. Those chosen undergo extensive background investigations to determine suitability for appointment. All special agent appointees must be citizens of the United States and be between 21 and 37 years of age when entering. Additionally, you must sign a mobility agreement, which indicates a willingness to accept a reassignment to any location in the future.

Fish and game wardens don't just work with fish and game. They spend a lot of time working with other officials and with members of the general public. Therefore, to succeed in this work, you must have good communication skills and enjoy working with people as much as caring for animals.

EXPLORING

Beth Ullenberg suggests you "stay in school, get a college education, and be willing to work summer jobs and even volunteer to gain experience." Doing volunteer work at a fish and wildlife facility is an excellent way to get some experience in this field and to see if you want to pursue a career in the area. Volunteering or working during the summer for the U.S. Fish and Wildlife Service would be the ideal, but serving with other environmental organizations can be useful as well. College students—and even students at select high schools—can apply for formal internships with various wildlife agencies. These can usually provide college (or possibly high school) credit and may even pay a small stipend.

Another easy way to explore this field is by simply getting outdoors. Take a hike, or spend time in a park observing the trees and wildlife. See if your family can plan an outdoors adventure. Ullenberg was active in the Girl Scouts when she was growing up, and enjoyed "many outdoor experiences through this organization" as well as through fishing trips with her family.

EMPLOYERS

The U.S. Fish and Wildlife Service employs over 7,500 men and women with diverse skills and backgrounds. Numerous jobs are also found with other agencies of the Department of the Interior, such as the National Park Service. Individual states also have positions in this area; contact your local state government, especially the state's park association, to find out about available positions. For instance, in Illinois you might contact the Illinois Department of Natural Resources.

STARTING OUT

The U.S. Fish and Wildlife Service fills jobs in various ways, including promoting or reassigning current employees, transferring employees from other federal agencies, rehiring former federal employees, or hiring applicants from outside the federal service. Applicants may also be hired to fill summer jobs. Applications for these positions must be submitted during a specified period—usually sometime between January and April of each year. The number and types of temporary positions vary from year to year. Contact the regional office nearest you to learn about current opportunities.

For information about specific Fish and Wildlife Service job openings, contact the Office of Personnel Management (http://www.opm.gov) and locate an office near you. Career planning and placement directors at colleges and universities can supply career information and training opportunities. Also, state employment or job services offices maintain listings of federal position vacancies. These offices can help you obtain the necessary forms to apply for jobs or direct you to sources for additional information.

You can also find job listings at USAJOBS (http://www.usajobs.opm.gov), a job bank for the U.S. government.

ADVANCEMENT

Prospects for advancement in this field improve greatly if fish and game wardens are willing to relocate. While they certainly can be promoted within their own facility, relocation opens up the possibility of taking a higher position whenever one opens up at any U.S. Fish and Wildlife Service location around the country.

EARNINGS

Like all federal employees, those who work for the U.S. Fish and Wildlife Service earn salaries as prescribed by law. Service employees are classified either as general schedule (GS) or as wage grade (WG). General schedule employees, the professional, technical, administrative, and clerical workers, receive annual salaries based on their GS grades (1 through 15). GS-5 salaries in 2008 ranged from $29,656 to $38,641. GS-7 salaries ranged from $33,057 to $42,290. GS-9 salaries ranged from $44,934 to $58,549. There are some areas in the United States that have an additional geographic locality pay.

In the wide variety of positions available at the U.S. Fish and Wildlife Service, salaries range from $18,000 all the way up to $91,000 for more advanced positions. Law enforcement positions, especially special agents, receive higher salaries because of the danger inherent in their jobs.

WORK ENVIRONMENT

With a number of different positions available, the work environment for each, of course, varies substantially. Wildlife inspectors, conservation police, or special agents generally spend a great deal of time outdoors, sometimes in remote areas, perhaps pursuing wildlife criminals. But they also need to spend time indoors, preparing

Educational Qualifications for Federal Wildlife Inspectors

GS-5: Four-year course of study above high school, leading to a bachelor's degree or three years of work-related experience, one year of which was at least equivalent to GS-4.

GS-7: One full academic year of graduate-level education or law school or superior academic achievement, or one year of specialized experience at least equivalent to GS-5.

GS-9: Two full academic years of graduate-level education or master's, LL.B., or J.D., or one year of specialized experience at least equivalent to GS-7.

detailed reports of their investigations and seeking additional information through research and other investigative techniques.

A refuge ranger or manager will divide his or her work time between indoor and outdoor activities. The various types of biologists will also spend time both indoors and outdoors, as their particular job dictates. All of these employees, however, will have a passion for the land and animal life, a dedication to preserving the environment, and the desire to make a difference in effecting positive changes. It can be very rewarding work in terms of personal satisfaction and sense of accomplishment. Very few of these jobs are of the nine-to-five variety, though; most require putting in extra hours.

OUTLOOK

As concern about the environment and wildlife grows, so too will the need for professional wildlife conservationists. Jobs with federal, state, and local agencies depend on the interests of the administration that is in power at the time. Administrations that lean more toward environmental issues will focus more on environmental rules and regulations, and may tend to provide more funding and support for wildlife conservation efforts. Beth Ullenberg thinks that "the future looks great!" She says, "Americans, [now] more than ever, realize the importance of protecting, conserving, and valuing our relationship with the natural world. They are more willing to conserve and support what they love."

FOR MORE INFORMATION

To learn more about wildlife conservation careers and related employment opportunities, contact the following organizations:

U.S. Fish and Wildlife Service
Department of the Interior
1849 C Street, NW
Washington, DC 20240-0001
Tel: 800-344-9453
http://www.fws.gov

U.S. National Park Service
Department of the Interior
1849 C Street, NW
Washington, DC 20240-0001
Tel: 202-208-6843
http://www.nps.gov

Foresters

OVERVIEW

Foresters protect and manage forest resources, one of our greatest natural assets, through various biological techniques. Using their specialized knowledge of tree biology and ecology, wood science, and manufacturing processes, they manage forests for timber production, protect them from fire and pest damage, harvest mature forests, and re-establish new forests after harvesting.

HISTORY

Not so long ago, forests were considered a hindrance to farming, a barrier to settlement, and a surplus commodity of minimal value to a small population of settlers. No profession existed to protect and manage the forests. By the mid-19th century, however, as the U.S. population grew and land clearing increased, people with foresight realized that forests were becoming more valuable and, unless protected, might disappear entirely. Laws enacted by the federal and state governments around that period helped to slow down forest destruction. At the same time, opening the Western territories to farming allowed forests to reclaim marginal farms abandoned in the East.

In 1900 seven individuals founded the Society of American Foresters. Back then they embodied practically the whole profession of forestry. By 1905 the U.S. Forest Service was established within the Department of Agriculture. Two years later, the Forest Service assumed responsibility for managing the newly established national forests.

Today there are 155 national forests and 20 grasslands. Each forest is divided into ranger districts, of which there are more than 600. Each district is run by a staff of 10 to 100 people, depending on the district's size. Not all of the country's forestland, however, is owned by the federal government. Many forests are owned by states and municipalities, and more than 50 percent of the country's forested land is privately owned. These non-federally owned forest areas amount to approximately 500 million acres and account for about 20 percent of the country's landmass. Because of the growing awareness that forest resources need to be managed wisely, the forestry profession has developed rapidly. Foresters and forestry technicians are charged with protecting the nation's forests from fire, insects,

Forest Facts

- Americans come into contact with more than 10,000 items each day that originated in forests.
- Most forest fires are now detected by aircraft or closed-circuit television, rather than the traditional lookout towers.
- The largest forest area in the United States is the Central Hardwood Forest.
- Most hardwoods are deciduous, which means they lose their leaves each fall. Most softwoods are evergreens, which means they lose only some of their needles each year and remain green year-round.
- Older, slower-growing trees and drought- or fire-damaged trees are most vulnerable to attack by disease and insects.
- The Society of American Foresters, founded in 1900, is the largest professional forestry society in the world.

and diseases; managing them for wood crops, water, wildlife, and forage; preserving their beauty and making them accessible; and training others to carry on their work.

THE JOB

Foresters do much of their work outdoors, especially during the early part of their careers. Ralph Unversaw, a district forester for the state of Indiana, still spends most of his time outdoors. "Normally, I spend about four days out of a five-day workweek outside, and the fifth inside trying to catch up on paperwork," he says. Most of Unversaw's job involves working with private woodland owners to manage their properties. "My job is to promote forest management," he says. "If they want to do some sort of timber management, I can advise them on planting, selecting trees for harvest, and harvesting."

Beginning foresters perform many duties. They may map areas of a forest and estimate the amounts of resources (such as timber, game shelter, and food, water, and forage for cattle and sheep) that they provide. They may also determine areas that need intervention, which can include planting trees, scattering seed from helicopters, controlling disease or insects, thinning dense forest stands, or pruning trees to produce better lumber or plywood. They may monitor stands of trees to ensure healthy growth and determine the best time for harvesting. They may layout logging roads or roads to lakes and recreational facilities and create the plans for building wilderness areas. Foresters may supervise crews doing all these jobs and inspect their work after it is done.

Foresters select and mark trees to be cut and check on the cutting and removal of the logs and pulpwood. They may be in charge of the lookouts, patrols, and pilots who detect fires and may lead crews that fight fires. They also sometimes oversee the operation of recreational areas, collect fees, issue permits, give talks to groups of campers, find lost hikers, and rescue climbers and skiers.

Even for foresters in the early stages of their careers, however, the work is not all outdoors. They must record the work done in the forest on maps and in reports. They use computers, data-processing equipment, and aerial photography to assist in this process. Although most beginning foresters do most of their work outside, some do work primarily indoors, in the technical laboratories and factories of wood-using industries. They may work in sawmills, plywood and hardboard plants, pulp and paper mills, wood-preserving plants, and furniture factories. These foresters are specialists in wood technology or pulp and paper technology. Many forest scientists work in laboratories and greenhouses, as well as in the forests, to learn how trees and forests grow.

Forests offer many benefits and can be used for many purposes. To maximize these benefits, foresters must not only know a great deal about the forest resources, but also be able to explain technical information to people, and secure their cooperation. From the beginning of their careers, foresters can expect to be called on to speak before various groups, from elementary school classes to service clubs and meetings of scientific societies. While not all foresters are in frequent contact with the public, they all eventually discover that their advancement depends on their ability to work with other people. "In my job, I have to do a lot of public relations-type work," says Unversaw. "I provide a lot of educational programs to the public—both to youth and to adults."

Much of the work that foresters do involves applying scientific knowledge and theory to actual practices in the field. Some foresters specialize in one or two of the basic sciences. In fact, some foresters are engaged in research that delves deeply into the fundamental physical and biological sciences. They work in laboratories with modern devices and equipment.

The scientific knowledge of how forests live is the specialty of *silviculturists*, who practice the art of establishing or reproducing forests, regulating their makeup, and influencing their growth and development along predetermined lines. The art of silviculture and the principles of economics and finance are the foundations of forest preservation and management.

One branch of forestry, known as forest engineering or logging engineering, combines forestry and engineering. Work in this field includes the design and construction of roads, bridges, dams, and buildings in forest areas. The design, selection, and installation of equipment for moving logs and pulpwood out of the forest is the special field of the *logging*, or *forest, engineer*. Forest and logging engineers might be graduates of schools of forestry that offer courses in this specialty, or they might have been trained as civil, mechanical, or electrical engineers.

Another type of specialist, the *forest ecologist*, conducts research to find out how forests are affected by changes in environmental conditions, such as soil, light, climate, altitude, and animal populations.

Other titles for foresters include forest pathologist, forestry consultant, forest supervisor, and wood chemist.

Foresters use a number of tools to perform their jobs. Clinometers measure the heights, diameter tapes measure the diameters, and increment borers and bark gauges measure the growth of trees. Photogrammetry and remote sensing (aerial photographs taken from airplanes and satellites) are often used to map large forest areas and detect widespread trends of forest growth and land use. Computers are used extensively, both in the office and in the field, to store, retrieve, and analyze the information required to manage the forestland and its resources.

In most forestry organizations and groups, a great deal of physical work in the woods needs to be done. This work is usually performed by people with experience and aptitude but little formal education beyond high school, or by forest technicians who have graduated from one- or two-year programs in forest technicians' institutes or ranger schools.

REQUIREMENTS
Ralph Unversaw prepared for his career as a forester by first obtaining a bachelor's degree in forestry and wildlife management. The minimal educational requirement to enter this career is a bachelor's degree in forestry; however, some foresters combine three years of liberal arts education with two years of professional education in forestry and receive the degrees of bachelor of arts and master of forestry. The Society of American Foresters (SAF), the professional society to which most foresters belong, currently accredits 50 schools in the United States with programs leading to forestry degrees at the bachelor's and master's levels. These programs are found in 38 states, most of them associated with state universities. For a listing of accredited programs, visit the SAF's Web site (http://safnet.org/education).

High School
Course work that focuses on mathematics and sciences will provide you with a solid foundation for a college forestry program. Take algebra, geometry, and statistics as well as biology, chemistry, physics, and any science course that will teach you about ecology. English classes are also important, since part of your job is likely to include research, writing reports, and presenting your findings. In addition, take history, economics, and, if possible, agriculture classes, which will teach you about soils and plant growth, among other things.

Postsecondary Training
The courses of study in all accredited schools of forestry have the same fundamental components. To be accredited, a school must

offer a specified amount of instruction in four essential areas of study: forest management (the application of business methods and silvicultural principles to the operation of forest properties), forest ecology and biology (ecosystem management and physiological principles including fires, insects, diseases, wildlife, and weather), forest policy and administration (understanding legislative procedures and environmental regulations that influence management decisions), and forest measurements (the inventory process for quantifying forest resources such as timber amount and quality, wildlife habitat, water quality, and recreational potential). The courses in these four topics, which are generally concentrated in the junior and senior years, make up the professional portion of the forester's schooling.

To prepare for these subjects, you need to be grounded in mathematics, surveying, chemistry, physics, botany, zoology, soil science, economics, and geology. Moreover, to help develop the skills needed for self-education later in your career, you need basic courses in literature, social studies, and writing. All of these courses are organized in a program that fills the freshman and sophomore years largely with basic sciences and humanities.

Foresters also do fieldwork as a part of their university training. Some schools of forestry are so close to forests that regular three-hour or all-day laboratory sessions are conducted in the school forest. Following the sophomore year in many schools of forestry is a summer camp of eight to 11 weeks. This is basically a continuous laboratory period during which you take part in the life of the forest, and, under guidance of the faculty, accumulate experience on which to draw in your junior and senior professional courses. In addition, some schools of forestry require you to spend an entire summer working for a forestry organization such as the U.S. Forest Service, National Park Service, a state forest service, or a company in the forest industry. The employer usually reports back to the school on your progress.

In addition to the basic sciences and humanities and the four core forestry areas of study, elective courses are offered to enable you to specialize in such fields as forest or logging engineering, wood technology, range management, wildlife management, forest recreation, and watershed management.

Graduates of forestry schools who wish to specialize in a certain area or broaden their general knowledge of forestry or related fields may opt for graduate work at one of the forestry schools to earn master's degrees or doctorates.

Certification or Licensing

Voluntary certification is offered by SAF and requirements include having completed a professional level (bachelor's degree or higher) education program and having at least five years of professional forestry experience. Those who meet requirements receive the designation certified forester and must complete a certain amount of continuing education for certification renewal every three years.

Some states offer voluntary or mandatory licensing or registration for foresters, depending on state regulations. Check with SAF or your state directly to find out about specific statutes and regulations.

Other Requirements

Because of the nature of the work, the forester must often make decisions on the basis of incomplete knowledge. This means that you must be self-reliant and have a high degree of initiative. You should have an aptitude for science, curiosity, and a passion for the outdoors. Because trees grow slowly and the changes in forests are gradual, you must have greater-than-average patience and a firm conviction that the work you do is important. If you make mistakes or are careless, the results may not be apparent for many years. Therefore, you must be dependable and conscientious. While it is not necessary to be intensely athletic, being physically fit and having stamina are essential.

EXPLORING

One way to explore the field of forestry is to talk with someone already working as a forester or forestry technician. In some parts of the country, local chapters of the SAF invite prospective forestry students to some of their meetings and field trips. School guidance counselors may have literature and information on forestry careers. Also, colleges and universities that offer forestry degrees should have information packets for interested students.

If you live near forested areas you might be able to find summer or part-time jobs in forestry. Unskilled workers are sometimes used for certain tasks, and this type of work could serve as a good introduction to the field by providing valuable experience and offering a view of what the job of a forester is really like.

EMPLOYERS

Federal, state, and local governments are by far the largest employers of foresters. There are approximately 33,000 foresters and conservation scientists working in the United States today. Of those, more than 50 percent of all salaried employees work for the federal (mostly in the U.S. Department of Agriculture's Forest Service), state, and local governments. While there are forester positions in every state, the majority of them are concentrated in the West and Southeast.

Foresters also work in private industry or are self-employed as consulting foresters. For those who work in private industry, employers include logging and lumber companies, sawmills, and research and testing facilities. Consulting foresters usually work with private or corporate owners of woodlands to help them manage their forests in the best way possible.

STARTING OUT

Finding a forester position is challenging, according to Ralph Unversaw. "I was fairly lucky because there happened to be a job opening right when I applied," he says. "There just aren't that many foresters' jobs and the competition is tough."

Because the majority of foresters are employed by government agencies, forestry school graduates might first pursue this avenue of employment. Job seekers should check with their state and local governments for job listings, as well as with federal agencies such as the Forest Service, Bureau of Land Management, National Park Service, and Bureau of Indian Affairs. Beginning foresters are often hired for government jobs on the basis of competitive civil service examinations.

Other foresters work for private industry, primarily for companies that manage forestlands for lumber, pulpwood, and other products. Newly graduated foresters should check with their college's career services office for information on job opportunities. Reference sections of local libraries may contain directories of wood products manufacturers, pulp and paper mills, timber firms, and conservation groups, all of which may employ foresters. Finally, the Society of American Foresters maintains a list of resources for the forestry job-seeker.

ADVANCEMENT

Professional foresters who have graduated from university-level schools of forestry often begin their first job with work that is not at a fully professional level. They may, for example, do the elementary surveying involved in forest inventory or engineering projects, work in logging or construction crews, or act as supervisors of planting or insect control crews. In organizations with room for advancement, this training period is short and is meant to provide a real understanding of operations from the bottom up.

After such a training period, foresters usually move to positions with more responsibility. This almost always means an increase in office work and a corresponding decrease in the time spent on physical work in the field.

As foresters move on to positions of greater responsibility in a public or private forestry organization, they may be placed in a line position—where the forester supervises technicians and other foresters. At the lower levels, the forester in a line position might directly supervise two to five other foresters; at higher levels the forester may still oversee only a small number of people, but each of them, in turn, will be in charge of a small group of foresters. Success in a line position requires leadership qualities in addition to professional competence and knowledge.

Other foresters may move into research. In research work, the forester may begin as a laboratory assistant, work gradually into detailed research activities, and eventually move into leadership or administrative positions in forestry research. Some foresters who move into research choose to return to school for further education.

A Better Way to Plant

Foresters and woodland owners often renew harvested forest areas by planting seeds or seedlings of particular kinds of trees. These seedlings are usually grown in large nurseries and transplanted when they are old and hardy enough to survive. When companies first began replanting harvested forests, all of the planting was done by hand. Since the 1940s, however, the replanting has increasingly been conducted by a tree-planting machine.

As the planting machine is pulled behind a tractor, a plow-like blade cuts open a furrow in the ground. A forestry worker places the seedlings in the ground by hand, and wheels on the planting machine close the furrow around the seedling. Much faster than the old method of planting, machine planting allows a crew to plant thousands of seedlings in one day.

With an advanced degree, such as a master's or doctorate, comes more opportunity for advancement, as well as better pay.

EARNINGS

According to the U.S. Department of Labor, median annual earnings of foresters in 2008 were $53,750. Salaries ranged from less than $34,710 for the lowest paid 10 percent to more than $78,350 for the highest paid 10 percent.

In 2006 most bachelor's degree graduates entering the federal government as foresters, range managers, or soil conservationists started at $28,862 or $35,752, depending on academic records. Those with a master's degree started at $43,731 or $52,912, and those with doctorates could start at $63,417. Starting salaries for foresters in private industry are comparable to starting salaries in the federal government, but starting salaries in state and local governments are generally somewhat lower. Whether working for private industry or federal, state, or local governments, foresters' salaries depend on their number of years of education and their experience in the field. Workers in this industry usually receive a benefits package that includes health insurance, paid vacations, and sick leave.

WORK ENVIRONMENT

Foresters generally work a 40-hour week, although they must be prepared for overtime duty, particularly when emergency conditions arise. In the field, foresters encounter many different conditions, including snow, rain, freezing cold, or extreme heat. They may sometimes be faced with hazardous conditions, such as forest fires.

The day-to-day duties of a forester in the field are often strenuous. "The job can be physically demanding," Ralph Unversaw says. "There's often a lot of walking."

Foresters whose work is more research-centered may not find the physical requirements as demanding as they may be spending more time in the laboratory. Their workweek also tends to be more regular and their routines somewhat less varied.

Most who choose a career in this field love nature and the outdoors; for them, a great benefit is being able to work in a beautiful, natural setting, free from the confines of a desk job in an office. "It's a great job if you like to be outdoors and walk through the woods," Unversaw says. "That's what I like best about it."

OUTLOOK

According to the U.S. Department of Labor, employment of foresters is expected to grow more slowly than the average for all occupations through 2016. Budgetary limitations have led to cutbacks in federal programs, where employment is concentrated. Also, federal land management agencies, such as the Forest Service, have given less attention to timber programs and focused more on wildlife, recreation, and sustaining ecosystems. Foresters with experience and knowledge of these areas will have the edge in the job market. Also, a large number of foresters are expected to retire or leave the government for other reasons, resulting in some job openings through 2016.

There have been reductions in timber harvesting on public lands, most of which are located in the Northwest and California, also affecting job growth for private industry foresters. Opportunities will be better for foresters on privately owned land in the Southeast. Landowners will continue to need consulting foresters, as will private industries, such as paper companies, sawmills, and pulp wood mills.

FOR MORE INFORMATION

For information on forestry and forests in the United States, contact
American Forests
PO Box 2000
Washington, DC 20013-2000
Tel: 202-737-1944
Email: info@amfor.org
http://www.americanforests.org

For information on forestry careers in Canada, contact
Canadian Forestry Association
1027 Pembroke Street East
Ottawa, ON K8A 3M4 Canada
Tel: 866-441-4006
Email: cfa@canadianforestry.com
http://www.canadianforestry.com

For information on forestry careers, schools, and certification, contact
Society of American Foresters
5400 Grosvenor Lane
Bethesda, MD 20814-2198

Tel: 866-897-8720
Email: safweb@safnet.org
http://www.safnet.org

For information about government careers in forestry as well as information on national forests across the country, contact
USDA Forest Service
1400 Independence Avenue, SW
Washington, DC 20250-0003
Tel: 800-832-1355
http://www.fs.fed.us

Forestry Technicians

OVERVIEW

Forestry technicians work as members of a forest management team under the direction of a professional forester. They collect data and information needed to make decisions about resources and resource depletion. They also help plan, supervise, and conduct the operations necessary to maintain and protect forest growth, including harvesting, replanting, and marketing of forest products. Forestry technicians understand the inventory methods and management skills required to produce wood fiber and forest products. They help manage forests and wildlife areas and control fires, insects, and disease. Forestry technicians may also survey land, measure the output of forest products, and operate logging and log-handling equipment.

HISTORY

Forests have provided wood and timber for fuel, shelter, and other construction since the beginning of civilization. Early peoples used wood to build boats and rafts, as well as dwelling places. By the time of the Roman Empire, vast amounts of wood were being cut in many forested areas of Europe. Fortunately, most of these forests were large enough and grew back fast enough to supply the needs of the Europeans.

Eventually, however, with the development of machines that reduced the cost and increased the speed of cutting logs, forests were cut down faster than they could grow back. Realizing this, Europeans began to conserve and manage their forests. This marked the beginning of the science of forestry.

Forests covered about half of North America when its only inhabitants were Native Americans. Much of this forested area was not cleared until early settlers first cut down the forests so they could build shelters and farm the land. With the clearing of the forests, as well as natural destructive forces such as fire and disease, the woodlands began to be depleted faster than they could grow back. By the early 1900s, only about one-third of the United States was forested. It became evident that the United States needed to follow the methods of forest management and conservation already used in Europe, and the government enacted a series of conservation measures. As part of these measures, professional foresters, tree genetics experts, forest-culture research scientists, and forest management scientists were trained to work in government and private industry.

By about 1960, the forestry profession had a need for technical workers to perform duties that required a training level higher than the manually skilled forest workers yet lower than the professional foresters and scientists. Certain colleges began to offer two-year programs leading to an associate's degree in forest technology, and the position of forestry technician was developed and recognized by the Society of American Foresters (SAF). The demand for these technically trained workers grew rapidly, and technicians have now become an essential part of the management team in the production and conservation process.

THE JOB

Forestry technicians perform duties that require scientific training and skill, frequently doing work that was once performed by professional foresters. Most are employed in forestland management and administration; they may be involved in timber production, recreation, wildlife forage, water regulation, preservation for scientific studies and special uses, or a combination of these areas.

Nate Benson, a forestry technician employed by the National Park Service, is the leader of a prescribed fire module. The module, one

Fire: Friend or Foe?

Although we have traditionally viewed the effects of fire as harmful, if not deadly, to plant and animal life, this is not necessarily always the case. Research has shown that not all changes from fire are bad. In fact, fire can renew and invigorate aging forests and release nutrients into the soil that accelerate the succession of vegetation types.

As private businesses and government agencies have come to better understand fire, they have experimented with how to use it to benefit the land—specifically forestland. The U.S. Forest Service began intentionally burning some southern forests in the 1940s to create new, even-age growth of greater commercial value. In the 1950s and 1960s, the National Park Service experimented with controlled burns in Everglades National Park, and by the late 1970s, a dozen national parks were allowing controlled fires to burn.

What was once simply fire suppression has now become fire management, with fire being used as a tool to shape and protect our wildlands.

of only nine in the nation, uses fire as a forest management resource. "We ignite and manage fires for ecological, cultural, and hazard-fuel benefits," Benson says. "Many different ecosystems are dependent upon fire. You need to burn out the smaller trees to let the larger ones persist." Burning wildlands in a planned and controlled manner can also decrease the chances of an unplanned and uncontrolled forest fire. "If the understory gets too heavy, it becomes more of a fire hazard," Benson says. "You'll want to burn it off to reduce the fuel load."

While not all forestry technicians perform the same types of duties, their day-to-day work includes general activities for managing and harvesting a forest. The first major step in the cycle is planting trees to replace those that have been cut down, harvested, or lost to disease or fire. Technicians tend and care for maturing trees by thinning them to obtain the best growth, spraying them with pesticides when necessary, and protecting them from fire or other damage. Periodic measuring or scaling of trees to determine the amount of lumber they will produce is necessary in planning for harvesting and marketing.

A forestry technician sprays a mixture of water and a horticultural wax into hemlock trees to manage the woolly adelgid, an insect pest that kills hemlocks. *AP Photo/Knoxville News Sentinel, Clay Owen*

Harvesting and marketing the trees is the last step. In preparing for harvesting, access roads for logging machinery and trucks are planned, surveyed, and built, sometimes with the use of aerial photography. Technicians must understand the land surveys and be able to interpret aerial photographs. After harvesting is complete, the land is reconditioned and the cycle begins again.

The work of a forestry technician is more complicated than it was just a few decades ago. Equipment and methods used to detect, prevent, and fight tree diseases and parasites have developed rapidly, as has the machinery used for harvesting, with powerful log handlers and loaders now being commonly used.

A forestry technician's work includes many different kinds of activities. In addition to the various duties required for each step of the tree-growing cycle, each forest area is managed with a particular objective, which affects the specific duties of the technician. Because the management plan for each area differs, the nature of technicians' jobs varies considerably.

Benson spends about half of his time in the Great Smoky Mountains National Park, where he is based. The remainder of the time, he and his six-person crew travel to other forested areas, wherever they are needed. He says some of his days are spent in the office, setting up logistical needs, creating "burn plans" for various regions, and tending to basic administrative tasks. Other days he spends in the field.

"On a day in the field, we travel to a particular park service unit and play a variety of different roles in the burning," he says. "We may assist with ignition by using a drip torch, or we may be involved in holding the fire behind the fire line to contain it. We may also be monitoring the fire, taking weather and fire behavior observations." Benson says that depending upon the size and complexity of the unit to be burned, projects may take anywhere from a day to a week to complete.

Forestry technicians employed by the federal government, like Benson, may specialize in a specific area of forestry. More often, however, they work as assistants to professional foresters in research connected with watershed management, timber management, wildlife management, forest genetics, fire control, disease and insect control, recreational development, and other matters. Many communities also now employ forestry technicians in the management of their municipal watersheds and in their parks and recreation development programs.

Some forestry technicians are employed by private industry, where they "cruise" timber (measure the volume of standing trees to determine their lumber content), survey logging roads, prepare maps and charts, and mark trees for cutting or thinning.

Following are descriptions of specialized positions that are held by forestry technicians. These positions may be found within federal or state agencies or the private forestry industry. Each requires a different mix of skills and abilities.

Information and education technicians write news releases and act as public relations specialists in nature centers.

Survey assistants locate and mark boundary lines. They also assist in the clearing of forests and construction of logging roads, prepare maps of surveys, and work on land appraisal and acquisition problems for private, state, and federal employers.

Biological aides work in insect and disease prevention and control. They record and analyze data, run experiments under supervision, and prepare maps to show damage done to forests by parasites.

Technical research assistants gather and analyze field data to assist scientists in basic and applied research problems that relate to timber, watershed, and wildlife management.

Sawmill buyers purchase high-grade logs for milling and furniture manufacture.

Pulp buyers purchase pulp logs for use in paper mills and other pulp and paper companies.

Lumber inspectors and/or *graders* grade and calculate the volume of hardwood and softwood lumber at mills or in retail and wholesale yards.

Tree-nursery management assistants help operate and manage tree nurseries. They keep records, hire temporary personnel, and supervise tree production during planting season. These technicians may also run seed tests and analyze data, operate and maintain equipment, and help supervise forest planting-stock production.

Wildlife technicians conduct fieldwork for various game commissions and federal agencies engaged in fish and game preservation and management. They capture, tag, and track animals with radio collars to establish territories and animal survival records. Wildlife technicians also help take wildlife censuses and maintain daily crew records.

REQUIREMENTS

Nate Benson's educational path did not lead him immediately into forestry. After receiving a bachelor's degree in Latin American studies, he began working for the National Park Service on a seasonal basis. Because he enjoyed the work so much, he went back to school for a master's degree in forestry and became a forestry technician.

High School

The best way to enter this field is to graduate from a formal program in forest technology. Almost all forest technology programs require a high school diploma, and most require applicants to have taken two courses in advanced mathematics and one course in physics. Courses in chemistry, biology, earth sciences, and any other courses in natural resources are excellent choices. Because you will need good writing and public speaking skills, English and speech classes are also recommended.

Postsecondary Training

Whether at a technical institute or a junior or community college, prospective technicians usually take a two-year program to receive an associate's degree. The Society of American Foresters (SAF) gives recognition to schools that offer associate's degrees in forestry technology (or its equivalent). For a listing of recognized schools, visit the SAF's Web site (http://www.safnet.org).

Since forestry technicians must learn both scientific theory and applied-science practices, the technical program is a demanding one. It requires organized classroom study and considerable time in the laboratory or field. Students must learn about the kinds of trees and plants that grow in a forest, and how they relate to or affect other plants and wildlife. Technicians also learn about measuring and calculating the amount of lumber in a tree. This is called mensuration, or forest measurements.

Students in forestry technician programs take mathematics, communications, botany, engineering, and technical forestry courses. The specific types of forestry courses taken vary, depending upon the climate in a given locale and the nature of local forestry practice.

A typical first year's study in a two-year forestry program might include the following courses: elementary forest surveying, communication skills, technical mathematics, dendrology (tree identification), botany of forests, forest orientation, technical reporting, elementary forest measurements, applied silviculture (how plants relate to each other), forest soils, computer applications, and elementary business management.

A typical second year's courses might include the following: personnel management, forest business methods, timber harvesting, advanced forest surveying and map drafting, outdoor recreation and environmental control, wildlife ecology, elements of social science, forest products utilization, forest protection, forest insect and disease control, forest fire control, advanced forest measurements, and aerial photographic interpretation.

Since student technicians also need practical experience working in a forest to learn many of the aspects of their jobs, almost all forestry technician programs require actual work experience in forested areas. Some schools arrange summer jobs for students between the first and second years of study. Many forestry technician programs also own or use a small sawmill where students can learn the basic elements of sawmill operation.

A special feature of some programs is a second-year seminar that includes visits to tree nurseries, sawmills, paper mills, veneer mills, wallboard manufacturing plants, and furniture factories. These visits help students understand how forest products are processed, used, measured, and classified by levels of quality. They also give students a better understanding of different types of companies that employ forestry technicians.

Certification or Licensing

In some states, forestry technicians need to be licensed to perform certain duties. For example, those working with pesticides or chemicals must be trained and licensed in their use. Technicians who make surveys of land for legal public property records are also required to hold a license.

Other Requirements

Forestry technicians must have a genuine enthusiasm for outdoor work. "You need to enjoy working outside, to have the ability to work in often extreme weather conditions, and to love learning more about the resource you're working with," Nate Benson says. "It's a great opportunity to work outdoors and do something you enjoy."

Because the job is often tough and physically demanding, technicians should have good health and stamina. In dealing with dangerous or emergency situations, such as forest fires, technicians need the ability to think clearly and act calmly and efficiently.

Self-direction, without supervision, is an essential in the job. Technicians often work in rural and remote areas, where they may be isolated from a supervisor and other workers for days or weeks at a time. To be successful in this career, you must be self-sufficient, resourceful, and able to tolerate solitude.

Despite the remoteness of most forestry work, effective communication skills are extremely important. Technicians must deal with other workers, members of the public who use the forest for recreation, and conservationists who protect fish, game, and plant life. Technicians may also supervise and coordinate the activities of laborers and field workers. Communication skills also are needed to prepare oral and written reports.

Forestry technicians must be able to apply both theoretical knowledge and specialized occupational skills. They need to be familiar with certain principles of engineering, biology, mathematics, and statistics, and know how to operate a computer.

EXPLORING

There are a number of ways you can learn more about a career in forest technology. High school guidance counselors may be able to provide you with materials and information on the career. Community and technical colleges may also have career information centers or other services that can provide information. For information about what the actual day-to-day work is like, you might visit a park or public land area and talk with forestry technicians about the specifics of their jobs.

For even more hands-on information, you might consider getting a summer or part-time job in forestry-related work, such as timber harvesting, clearing, or planting operations. State forestry departments, federal agencies, private companies, or environmental groups are all potential sources of summer or part-time work. The National Wildlife Federation's *Conservation Directory* (http://www.nwf.org/conservationDirectory) lists names and addresses of state and federal land management agencies and other groups concerned with the environment.

EMPLOYERS

Approximately 34,000 forest and conservation technicians are employed in the United States. About 93 percent of all technicians work for federal and state governments. In the federal government, most jobs are in the U.S. Department of Agriculture's Forest Service or the Department of Interior's Bureau of Land Management. Opportunities in the federal government also exist with the Natural Resources Conservation Service, the National Park Service, and the U.S. Army Corps of Engineers.

State governments also employ forestry technicians to provide services to private forestland owners and to manage state forest lands. In many states, the Cooperative Extension Service and the Department of Natural Resources have forestry positions. County and municipal governments may also have forestry positions.

There are also a number of employment opportunities in the private sector. Technicians work with companies that manage forestlands for lumber, pulpwood, and other products. Companies that use forest products and suppliers of forestry equipment and materials also hire forestry technicians. Other employers include private estates, tree service companies, and forestry consulting firms.

STARTING OUT

For Nate Benson, a full-time job in forest technology was not easy to come by. "I worked seasonally for 10 years and went back to school to get my master's degree before I got a full-time position," he says. "Initially, it's hard to get career positions in federal land management agencies. You can work seasonally for a long time and not necessarily get a break."

Graduates of technical forestry programs have the best prospects for entering this profession. Although a two-year degree is not a requirement, you will find it much more difficult to find a job without one.

Technicians who have graduated from a college program usually learn about employment leads from their school's career services office, instructors, or guidance staff members. Students who have worked in forestry part time or during summers may be hired on a permanent basis after graduation. Working seasonally may also be a good way to break into the field.

If you choose to pursue a career in the private sector, you should apply directly to companies that employ forestry technicians.

 FORESTRY TERMS

age class   An age grouping of trees according to an interval of years, usually 20 years. A single age class would have trees that are within 20 years of the same age, such as 1–20 years or 21–40 years.

broadcast burn   A prescribed fire that burns a designated area. These controlled fires can reduce wildfire hazards, improve forage for wildlife and livestock, or encourage successful regeneration of trees.

crown height   The distance from the ground to the base of the crown of a tree.

ecosystem management   An ecological approach to natural resource management to assure productive, healthy ecosystems by blending social, economic, physical, and biological needs and values.

even-age management   Timber management actions that result in the creation of stands of trees in which the trees are essentially the same age.

intermediate cut   The removal of trees from a stand sometime between the beginning or formation of the stand and the regen-

ADVANCEMENT

Forestry technicians can advance in a number of different ways. Technicians who are federal employees advance to higher grades and better salaries after attaining a certain number of years of experience. According to Nate Benson, however, competition for advancement can be fierce. "In the Park Service, part of the problem you run into is that it's a wide-based pyramid, and there aren't that many positions to move into," he says. "It's pretty competitive."

Some advancement opportunities require additional schooling. For example, a forestry technician who wants to become a forester needs to complete a four-year degree program. Other forestry technicians advance by moving into research work. Following are potential positions to which a technician can advance.

eration cut. Types of intermediate cuts include thinning, release, and improvement cuttings.

ladder fuels   Vegetation located below the crown level of forest trees, which can carry fire from the forest floor to tree crowns. Ladder fuels may be low-growing tree branches, shrubs, or smaller trees.

litter (forest litter)   The freshly fallen or only slightly decomposed plant material on the forest floor. This layer includes foliage, bark fragments, twigs, flowers, and fruit.

multiple-use management   The management of all the various renewable surface resources of national forest lands for a variety of purposes, such as recreation, range, timber, wildlife and fish habitat, and watershed.

old growth   Old forests often containing several canopy layers, with a variety of tree sizes and species.

reforestation   The restocking of an area with forest trees, by either natural or artificial means (planting).

sanitation salvage   The removal of dead, damaged, or susceptible trees primarily to promote forest health and prevent the spread of pests or disease.

Timber cruisers supervise crews in the measurement of trees for volume computations. They keep records, run statistical analyses of volumes, and mark timber for sale. They recommend logging methods and use aerial photographs to locate future timber harvesting areas.

Forest-fire control technicians maintain fire control supplies in a central area and report fires by radio-telephone. They recruit, train, and supervise forest-fire wardens and crews, sometimes dispatching and serving as crew leaders in fire suppression. They also conduct investigations into the causes of fires. They also educate communities in fire prevention.

Refuge managers supervise work crews in game and fish management. They help plant food plots for wildlife and other plants for habitat improvement. They patrol restricted areas, conduct census studies, and make maps.

Sawmill managers supervise sawmills, oversee crew and production schedules, and keep payroll records.

Kiln operators supervise and control the kiln schedules for correct drying of lumber. They run drying tests and submit reports on loads of drying lumber.

Forest recreation technicians supervise the operation and maintenance of outdoor recreation facilities. They are responsible not only for tactful enforcement of rules but also for fire watches.

Assistant logging superintendents control harvesting and loading operations for timber sales. They help maintain safety, keep payroll and supply records, and write technical reports for superintendents.

Forestry consultants fill an increasingly important role in forestry by providing forestry services to people whose property or business does not require a permanent, full-time forester.

Experienced forestry technicians may also build rewarding careers in research. *Research technicians* perform many varied functions, such as obtaining data for computer analysis, helping develop new chemical fire retardants, and designing machines to prepare forest soils for planting. Research technicians work for private industries, large cities, or state and federal government agencies.

EARNINGS

Salary levels vary greatly depending on employer and area of forestry. According to the U.S. Department of Labor, median wages for forest and conservation technicians were $32,000 in 2008. The top 10 percent of forest and conservation technicians earned over

$51,810, and the bottom 10 percent earned less than $22,540 a year. Forestry technicians who worked for the federal government averaged $34,790 in 2008.

Those employed by government agencies typically earn less than technicians employed by private industries. Positions with the federal government tend to pay slightly higher wages than those in state governments.

Benefits usually include paid holidays, vacation and sick days, and insurance and retirement plans, although these vary by employer. Some employers offer part or full tuition reimbursement for job-related schooling.

WORK ENVIRONMENT

Working hours for forestry technicians are fairly normal. Most technicians work eight-hour days, five days a week. In case of fires or other unusual situations, however, longer hours may be necessary.

Some of the work is physically demanding. In addition, technicians working in the field may occasionally have to deal with hazardous conditions such as forest fires. "The job often involves hard, physical labor and strenuous work," says Nate Benson. "And there is always the chance of danger; although if you take the necessary precautions, you shouldn't get into trouble."

For many technicians, most of the working day is spent outdoors, even in unpleasant weather, in settings that are sparsely settled, primitive, and remote. Many forest areas do not have paved roads, and large areas have only a few roads or trails that are passable.

Technicians who work in laboratories or offices generally have well-lit, modern, and comfortable surroundings.

OUTLOOK

Employment of forest and conservation technicians is expected to show little or no change through 2016, according to the *Occupational Outlook Handbook*. Most job openings will result from technicians leaving the field or being promoted to other areas. Competition will be strong, though, so technicians with forestry technology and machinery management knowledge will have an advantage over less prepared applicants in the job market.

The increased awareness for protecting the environment will continue the demand for conservation and forestry workers, especially in state and local governments. Forestry technicians who have knowledge of urban forestry and geographic information systems will have especially strong employment opportunities. Budgetary constraints, however, will affect hiring, particularly at the federal and state levels of government.

Forest recreation is a promising area for future employment for forestry technicians. Ever-increasing numbers of people are enjoying the forests. These resources must be managed for the protection of the users, as well as of the resources themselves, and such management requires the expertise of foresters and forestry technicians.

In addition, new uses for wood and wood products are continually being found. Meeting this growing demand requires an increasing supply of timber and pulp. Forestry technicians who specialize in land management and the various aspects of logging and sawmill work will play a valuable role in assuring this supply. Research technicians who help find improved methods of planting, growing, and timber and pulp production will be needed in greater numbers.

FOR MORE INFORMATION

For information on forests in the United States and to read selections from American Forests *magazine, visit*

American Forests
PO Box 2000
Washington, DC 20013-2000
Tel: 202-737-1944
Email: info@amfor.org
http://www.americanforests.org

Find information on conservation, jobs, and the online Conservation Directory, *a directory of environmental groups around the country and the world, at the NWF Web site.*

National Wildlife Federation (NWF)
11100 Wildlife Center Drive
Reston, VA 20190-5362
Tel: 800-822-9919
http://www.nwf.org

For a list of recognized associate degree programs and other information on careers in forestry, contact

Society of American Foresters
5400 Grosvenor Lane
Bethesda, MD 20814-2198
Tel: 866-897-8720

Email: safweb@safnet.org
http://www.safnet.org

For information about government careers in forestry, contact
USDA Forest Service
1400 Independence Avenue, SW
Washington, DC 20250-0003
Tel: 800-832-1355
http://www.fs.fed.us

Groundwater Professionals

QUICK FACTS

School Subjects
Earth science
Mathematics

Personal Skills
Communication/ideas
Technical/scientific

Work Environment
Indoors and outdoors
Primarily one location

Minimum Education Level
Bachelor's degree

Salary Range
$44,410 to $71,450 to
$105,010+

Certification or Licensing
Voluntary

Outlook
Much faster than the average

OVERVIEW

Groundwater professionals are different types of scientists and engineers concerned with water supplies beneath the earth's surface. For example, they search for new water sources and ensure safe water supply. They may specialize in either underground water or surface water.

HISTORY

In addition to the water that can be seen on the surface of the earth, such as lakes, streams, rivers, ponds, canals, and oceans, there is water under the ground, known as groundwater. Groundwater includes underground streams and aquifers, which are layers of water-bearing porous rock or sediment. People have been tapping into various groundwater sources for centuries, using the water for everything from drinking to irrigation.

Artesian wells, for example, are used to provide water (including drinking water) in some parts of the world. They are created by boring down into aquifers; the resulting pressure causes water in the aquifer to rise up in the well. Australia has the world's biggest artesian well system; in the United States, artesian systems supply water to parts of the Great Plains and the East Coast.

Like other natural resources, groundwater has been the focus of increasing attention in the United States since the 1970s. The U.S. government has recognized threats to this vital supply of water and passed laws to protect it. At first, people in the field and in related fields were called on to adapt their skills to meeting the new regulations. In recent years, especially as the regulations have gotten more technical and complex, demand for people who specialize in groundwater science has risen dramatically.

A look at the groundwater situation in one state, Florida, demonstrates some of the potential problems. The groundwater in many areas is located not very far beneath the surface—just a few feet, in some cases. A surging population is drawing heavily on these supplies, threatening to use them faster than they can replenish themselves. Rapid development (farming, mining, construction, industry) offers high potential for disrupting the vulnerable groundwater.

Also, in some cases, beneath the Florida aquifers that carry good water are aquifers that carry poor-quality (high in sulfates) water. Drawing down too far into the aquifers that have good water might accidentally pull up the bad water from deeper aquifers, or, worse, draw in saltwater from the coast. And once saltwater gets in, that aquifer is probably lost as a source of drinking water.

Another groundwater hazard is the possibility of a fuel, chemical, or other spill on the ground. Hazardous chemicals in these substances can soak through the soil and reach the groundwater, contaminating it. Even good-quality groundwater usually is treated before it is used (although in some places, like outlying rural areas, people drink untreated groundwater, taking it right out of the ground). Regular water-treatment facilities are not designed to handle removal of hazardous substances. That requires special steps, is usually more difficult and expensive than cleaning surface water, and sometimes does not work.

This is, in fact, a national concern. Today, according to the Environmental Protection Agency, almost 50 percent of the U.S. population relies on groundwater for domestic use. At the same time, better methods for detecting contaminants have revealed that contamination of groundwater is more extensive than was previously known.

Legislation (including the Resource Conservation and Recovery Act; the Comprehensive Environmental Response, Compensation, and Liability Act; the Superfund Amendments and Reauthorization

Act; and the Safe Drinking Water Act) mandates the cleanup, monitoring, and protection of the nation's groundwater supplies. This direction was strengthened by later amendments to such laws. Recent stricter regulations applying to landfills, for example, acknowledge the potential risks of these operations to groundwater. In particular, seepage from landfills can get into the groundwater and contaminate it. New landfills must have double liners and other features to help prevent seepage; existing landfills have new rules about closing and capping the landfill to try to stop or minimize seepage. Groundwater monitoring equipment is used to take constant readings of the area's groundwater and determine if any seepage is occurring.

The special problems of groundwater, people's reliance on it, and the laws passed to protect it all have contributed to the growing need for groundwater professionals. Groundwater work is part of the water quality management segment of the environmental industry, which accounts for about one-quarter of all spending on the environment, according to the Environmental Careers Organization.

 WORDS TO KNOW

aquifer   A water-bearing layer of permeable rock, soil, or unconsolidated glacial overburden.

bailer   Used for collecting water samples from wells. Usually a plastic tube, open at either end, with check valves. The check valves seal as the bailer is pulled out of water, thereby collecting samples.

DNAPL   Dense nonaqueous phase liquid, or a liquid that tends to sink in water without readily dissolving. DNAPLs include solvents and some oils. Because DNAPLs sink in aquifers, they can be difficult to locate and remove.

LNAPL   Light nonaqueous phase liquid, or gasoline or oil that does not tend to sink in water.

NAPL   Nonaqueous phase liquid, or an oil.

plume   An area of contamination within groundwater.

THE JOB

No one really has the title of groundwater professional; instead, it describes any of a number of different positions within the groundwater industry. These include different types of scientists, engineers, and technicians employed in government, private industry, and nonprofit organizations at various tasks designed to ensure safe, effective, and lawful use of groundwater supplies. In earlier times, geologists were often called upon to do groundwater work, and they continue to be important players in the field today. Geology is the science of the earth's history, composition, and structure. Specialties in the groundwater field today include hydrogeology and hydrology. *Hydrogeologists* study the science of groundwater supplies. *Hydrologists* study underground and surface water and its properties, including how water is distributed and how it moves through land. Other professionals in the groundwater industry include chemists, geological engineers, water quality technicians, computer modelers, environmental engineers, chemists, bioremediation specialists, petroleum geologists, and mining engineers.

Employers of groundwater professionals include local water districts, government agencies, consulting firms, landfill operations, private industry, and others with a stake in successful groundwater management. What groundwater professionals do depends on the employer.

Local or regional authorities usually are responsible for ensuring a safe and adequate water supply for people in the area. For example, any time people want to make a new use of water or do something that might affect water in the area (like building a road, drilling a well, or laying a sewer), they have to get a permit. Before it will issue a permit, the authority has groundwater professionals check the site and decide if the use is safe. Typically, geologists do the necessary fieldwork, while engineers obtain the actual permits.

For a local or regional authority, groundwater professionals might help locate new sources of water in the area, which typically involves surveying the area, drilling for samples, and measuring the capacity of any water reserves found. They find the source of the groundwater and determine its ability to replenish itself if tapped for use, decide how the water would best be used, and make a recommendation to the authority. If the authority approves, a new well system is designed to tap the groundwater, and wells are drilled.

States are big employers of groundwater professionals. What groundwater professionals do for a state depends greatly on what part of the country it is in. The mapping of known groundwater supplies, often using computer modeling to show groundwater flow and possible effects of contamination, is often part of their efforts.

For both state and local or regional authorities, combating the effects of contamination is a critical task. The nature and extent of contamination, combined with the geologic and hydrologic characteristics of the surrounding land, determine whether the water supply is permanently tainted or can be made usable again in the future. Groundwater professionals design systems to reduce or stop contamination.

Consulting firms are another big employer. Regulations for waste treatment and disposal are becoming more and more strict, and that means that more technical expertise is required. Lacking that expertise themselves, many waste generators in the public and private sectors turn to consulting firms for help. Consultants may be called in to help with a hazardous waste cleanup around a landfill, at a Superfund site (an abandoned hazardous waste site), or at another cleanup, or they may help a private industrial company devise a system to handle its waste. Groundwater professionals can be very useful to such consulting firms. For example, if a landfill is leaking waste into a source of groundwater, a groundwater specialist could devise solutions, such as digging new drainage systems for the landfill or building new containment facilities. A groundwater professional with a consulting firm might work close to home or travel to job sites around the country or even around the world.

REQUIREMENTS
High School
At the high school level, you can prepare for a career in groundwater work by taking a lot of science and math classes. Technology is important in this field, so make sure you have computer skills. Also, focus on developing your writing and speech skills. Reports, proposals, memos, scientific papers, and other forms of written and verbal communication are likely to be part of your job as a groundwater professional.

Postsecondary Training
A bachelor's degree is the minimum requirement for being a professional in this field. According to the Environmental Careers Organization, geology, civil engineering, and chemistry are the

most common undergraduate degrees in this field today. Other appropriate majors are engineering, geology, hydrogeology, geophysics, petroleum geology, mining engineering, and other related degrees. Another possibility is a degree in hydrology. Appropriate course work at the undergraduate level includes chemistry, physics, calculus, atmospheric science, aquatic biology, groundwater geology, groundwater hydrology, engineering hydrology, soil science, fluid mechanics, and water resource management and conservation. Classes in environmental regulation and policy can be helpful. It is also a good idea to learn how to do computer modeling, mapping, and related tasks. Undergraduate degrees are sufficient for getting a job doing activities such as on-site sampling and measurement.

A degree in hydrogeology is usually obtained at the master's level. This degree and some experience will place you among the most sought-after workers in the environmental industry.

Certification or Licensing
Some certification programs have been developed to measure experience and knowledge of groundwater science. Both the American Institute of Hydrology and the National Ground Water Association offer voluntary certification programs.

Other Requirements
Patience, persistence, curiosity, attention to detail, and good analytic skills are all useful for a groundwater professional. You may work as part of a team and have people to answer to, whether a supervisor, the government, a client, or all three. Familiarity with numerous and often complex regulations may also be required in the job.

EXPLORING
A part-time or summer job with a consulting firm is an excellent way to learn more about this job and the industry. Use an Internet search engine to find hydrology and environmental science consulting firms near you. Volunteering for a nonprofit environmental organization might also be an option.

EMPLOYERS
Employers of groundwater professionals include local water districts, government agencies, consulting firms, landfill operations,

private industry, and others with a stake in successful groundwater management.

STARTING OUT

There are many ways to find openings in the industry. Professional associations such as the National Ground Water Association often have career sections on their Web sites where they list jobs and upcoming conferences and networking events (http://careers.ngwa. org/home/index.cfm?site_id=7312). Other job-hunting options include the classified sections of newspapers and professional journals. New graduates can also look for work at state employment offices, local or regional water authorities, or the local branches of federal agencies.

ADVANCEMENT

Beginning groundwater professionals are likely to do things like sampling and measuring work. Advancement will follow different paths, depending on where the groundwater professional works and his or her skills and interests. Those with an advanced degree, years of experience, and a commitment to continuing education will have better opportunities to move ahead.

Advancement in private consulting firms will likely include promotion to an administrative position, which will mean spending more time in the office, dealing with clients, and directing the activities of other groundwater specialists and office staff. Those working for a local, regional, state, or federal organization may rise to an administrative level, meeting with planning commissions, public interest groups, legislative bodies, and industry groups.

Another option is for groundwater professionals to strike out on their own. With some experience, ambitious professionals can start their own consulting firm.

EARNINGS

Groundwater professionals are among the highest paid professionals in the water industry. The U.S. Department of Labor reports that median annual earnings of hydrologists were $71,450 in 2008. The lowest paid 10 percent earned less than $44,410, and the highest paid 10 percent earned $105,010 or more.

Benefits depend on the employer. They might include paid vacation, sick days, personal days, health and dental insurance, tuition reimbursement, retirement savings plans, and use of company vehicles.

WORK ENVIRONMENT

Fieldwork might mean going to natural areas to survey the geophysical characteristics of a site. Groundwater professionals might need to take water samples from the monitoring wells near a gas station, fuel storage facility, landfill, sewage treatment plant, or manufacturing company. They may oversee the digging of a new well system or check to see how a new well system is running. Although responsibilities depend on a professional's specific job, some work outside of the office and outdoors is frequently part of the job.

In addition to fieldwork, groundwater professionals spend time working in offices. Some professionals, in fact, may spend most or all of their time indoors. Conditions in offices vary by employer, but offices are generally equipped with state-of-the-art technology. Most groundwater professionals work a 40-hour week, depending on project deadlines or unexpected developments.

OUTLOOK

The field of groundwater science remains a promising career choice for motivated, intelligent students. The *Occupational Outlook Handbook* predicts that employment for hydrologists and environmental scientists will grow much faster than the average for all occupations through 2016. The continued growth of our nation's population makes finding and remediating groundwater supplies an even more pressing issue in the 21st century. Private industry must continue to comply with stricter government regulations, including those related to keeping groundwater safe from contamination. Local, regional, and state authorities need to map, develop, and protect their groundwater supplies. Consultants need the specific expertise that groundwater professionals can offer, for clients both in the United States and abroad. Research is needed to develop new ways to treat contaminated groundwater, to prevent spills or leaks, and to develop systems that will make the most of groundwater supplies. All of this means work for groundwater professionals for the near future.

FOR MORE INFORMATION

For the brochure Careers in the Geosciences *and listings of geoscience departments, visit the institute's Web site.*
American Geological Institute
4220 King Street
Alexandria, VA 22302-1502
Tel: 703-379-2480
http://www.agiweb.org

For information on the hydrologic sciences, contact
American Geophysical Union
2000 Florida Avenue, NW
Washington, DC 20009-1277
Tel: 800-966-2481
Email: service@agu.org
http://www.agu.org

For information on certification, student chapters, and related organizations, contact
American Institute of Hydrology
Engineering D - Mail Code 6603
Southern Illinois University Carbondale
1230 Lincoln Drive
Carbondale, IL 62901-4335
Tel: 618-453-7809
Email: aih@engr.siu.edu
http://www.aihydrology.org/

For information on grants, internships, and issues in geoscience, contact
Geological Society of America
PO Box 9140
Boulder, CO 80301-9140
Tel: 888-443-4472
Email: gsaservice@geosociety.org
http://www.geosociety.org

For information on certification, contact
National Ground Water Association
601 Dempsey Road
Westerville, OH 43081-8978

Tel: 800-551-7379
Email: ngwa@ngwa.org
http://www.ngwa.org

For general information about groundwater, visit the following Web sites:
U.S. Environmental Protection Agency
http://www.epa.gov/safewater

U.S. Geological Survey
http://water.usgs.gov/ogw

Naturalists

School Subjects
Biology
Earth science
English

Personal Skills
Communication/
 ideas
Technical/scientific

Work Environment
Primarily outdoors
One location with some
 travel

Minimum Education Level
Bachelor's degree

Salary Range
$29,656 to $42,290 to
$70,844+

Certification or Licensing
None available

Outlook
Little change or more
 slowly than the average

OVERVIEW

The primary role of *naturalists* is to educate the public about the environment and maintain the natural environment on land specifically dedicated to wilderness populations. Their primary responsibilities are preserving, restoring, maintaining, and protecting a natural habitat. Among the related responsibilities in this job are teaching, public speaking, writing, giving scientific and ecological demonstrations, and handling public relations and administrative tasks. Naturalists may work in a variety of environments, including private nature centers; local, state, and national parks and forests; wildlife museums; and independent nonprofit conservation and restoration associations. Some of the many job titles a naturalist might hold are *wildlife manager, fish and game warden, fish and wildlife officer, land steward, wildlife biologist,* and *environmental interpreter. Natural resource managers, wildlife conservationists,* and *ecologists* sometimes perform the work of naturalists.

HISTORY

Prior to the 17th century, there was little support for environmental preservation. Instead, wilderness was commonly seen as a vast resource to be controlled. This view began to change during the early years of the industrial revolution, when new energy resources were utilized, establishing an increasing need for petroleum, coal, natural gas, wood, and water for hydro-powered energy. In England and France, for example, the rapid depletion of natural forests caused by the increased use of timber for powering the new industries led to demands for forest conservation.

The United States, especially during the 19th century, saw many of its great forests razed, huge tracts of land leveled for open-pit mining and quarrying, and increased disease with the rise of air pollution from the smokestacks of factories, home chimneys, and engine exhaust. Much of the land damage occurred at the same time as a dramatic depletion of wildlife, including elk, antelope, deer, bison, and other animals of the Great Plains. Some types of bear, cougar, and wolf became extinct, as did several kinds of birds, such as the passenger pigeon. In the latter half of the 19th century, the U.S. government set up a commission to develop scientific management of fisheries, established the first national park (Yellowstone National Park in Wyoming), and set aside the first forest reserves. The modern conservation movement grew out of these early steps.

States also established parks and forests for wilderness conservation. Parks and forests became places where people, especially urban dwellers, could acquaint themselves with the natural settings of their ancestors. Naturalists, employed by the government, institutions of higher education, and various private concerns, were involved not only in preserving and exploring the natural reserves but also in educating the public about the remaining wilderness.

Controversy over the proper role of U.S. parks and forests began soon after their creation (and continues to this day), as the value of these natural areas for logging, recreation, and other human activities conflicts with the ecological need for preservation. President Theodore Roosevelt, a strong supporter of the conservation movement, believed nevertheless in limited industrial projects, such as dams, within the wilderness areas. Despite the controversy, the system of national parks and forests expanded throughout the 20th century. Today, the Agriculture and Interior Departments, and, to a lesser extent, the Department of Defense, have conservation

A naturalist reviews treatment plans to protect trees in Chimney Rock Park in North Carolina from insect pests. *AP Photo/Chuck Burton*

responsibilities for soil, forests, grasslands, water, wildlife, and federally owned land.

In the 1960s and early 1970s the hazards posed by pollution to both humans and the environment highlighted the importance of nature preservation and public education. Federal agencies were established, such as the Environmental Protection Agency, the Council on Environmental Quality, and the National Oceanic and Atmospheric Administration. Crucial legislation was passed, including the Wilderness Act (1964) and the Endangered Species Act (1969). Naturalists have since been closely involved with these conservation efforts and others, shouldering the responsibility to communicate to the public the importance of maintaining diverse ecosystems and to help restore or balance ecosystems under threat.

THE JOB

Because of the impact of human populations on the environment, virtually no area in the United States is truly wild. Land and the animal populations require human intervention to help battle against the human encroachment that is damaging or hindering wildlife. Naturalists work to help wildlife maintain or improve their hold in the world.

The work can be directly involved in maintaining individual populations of animals or plants, overseeing whole ecosystems, or promoting the work of those who are directly involved in the maintenance of the ecosystem. Fish and wildlife officers (or fish and game wardens) work to preserve and restore the animal populations, including migratory birds that may only be part of the environment temporarily. Wildlife managers and range conservationists oversee the combination of plants and animals in their territories.

Fish and wildlife officers and wardens study, assist, and help regulate the populations of fish, hunted animals, and protected animals throughout the United States. They may work directly in the parks and reserves, or they may oversee a region within a particular state, even if there are no parklands there. Fish and game wardens control the hunting and fishing of wild populations to make sure that the populations are not overharvested during a season. They monitor the populations of each species off-season as well as make sure the species is thriving but is not overpopulating and running the risk of starvation or territory damage. Most people hear about the fish and game wardens when a population of animals has overgrown its territory and needs either to be culled (selectively hunted) or moved.

Usually this occurs with the deer population, but it can also apply to predator animals such as the coyote or fox, or scavenger animals such as the raccoon. Because the practice of culling animal populations arouses controversy, the local press usually gives wide coverage to such situations.

The other common time to hear about wildlife wardens is when poaching is uncovered locally. Poaching can be hunting or fishing an animal out of season or hunting or fishing a protected animal. Although we think of poachers in the African plains hunting lions and elephants, poaching is common in the United States for animals such as mountain lions, brown bears, eagles, and wolves. Game wardens target and arrest poachers; punishment can include prison sentences and steep fines.

Wildlife managers, range managers, and conservationists work to maintain the plant and animal life in a given area. Wildlife managers can work in small local parks or enormous national parks. Range managers work on ranges that have a combination of domestic livestock and wild population. The U.S. government has leased and permitted farmers to graze and raise livestock on federally held ranges, although this program is under increasing attack by environmentalists. Range managers must ensure that both the domestic and wild populations are living side by side successfully. They make sure that the population of predatory wild animals does not increase enough to deplete the livestock and that the livestock does not overgraze the land and eliminate essential food for the wild animals. Range managers and conservationists must test soil and water for nutrients and pollution, count plant and animal populations in every season, and keep in contact with farmers using the land for reports of attacks on livestock or the presence of disease.

Wildlife managers also balance the needs of the humans using or traveling through the land they supervise and the animals that live in or travel through that same land. They keep track of the populations of animals and plants and provide food and water when it is lacking naturally. This may involve airdrops of hay and grain during winter months to deer, moose, or elk populations in remote reaches of a national forest, or digging and filling a water reservoir for animals during a drought.

Naturalists in all these positions often have administrative duties such as supervising staff members and volunteers, raising funds (particularly for independent nonprofit organizations), writing grant applications, taking and keeping records and statistics, and maintaining public relations. They may write articles for local or national publications to inform and educate the public about their location

Some Pioneer Naturalists

Ralph Waldo Emerson (1803–82), an American philosopher and author. He helped formulate and promote the philosophy known as Transcendentalism, which emphasizes the spiritual dimension in nature and in all persons.

Henry David Thoreau (1817–62), an American author. His *Walden; or, Life in the Woods* is a classic of American literature. It is an account of the two years he lived in a small cabin on the shore of Walden Pond near Concord, Massachusetts. In *Walden*, he vividly describes the changing seasons and other natural events and scenes that he observed.

Gilbert White (1720–93), an English minister. While pursuing his vocation in his native village of Selborne (southwest of London), White became a careful observer of its natural setting. He corresponded with important British naturalists and eventually published *The Natural History and Antiquities of Selborne*.

or a specific project. They may be interviewed by journalists for articles concerning their site or their work.

Nature walks are often given to groups as a way of educating people about the land and the work that goes into revitalizing and maintaining it. Tourists, schoolchildren, amateur conservationists and naturalists, social clubs, and retirees commonly attend these walks. On a nature walk, the naturalist may point out specific plants and animals, identify rocks, and discuss soil composition or the natural history of the area (including special environmental strengths and problems). The naturalist may even discuss the indigenous people of the area, especially in terms of how they adapted to the unique aspects of their particular environment. Because such a variety of topics may be brought up, the naturalist must be an environmental generalist, familiar with such subjects as biology, botany, geology, geography, meteorology, anthropology, and history.

Demonstrations, exhibits, and classes are ways that the naturalist can educate the public about the environment. For example, to help children understand oil spills, the naturalist may set up a simple demonstration showing that oil and water do not mix. Sometimes the natural setting already provides an exhibit for the naturalist. Dead fish, birds, and other animals found in a park may help demonstrate the natural life cycle and the process of decomposition. Instruction may also be given on outdoor activities, such as hiking and camping.

For some naturalists, preparing educational materials is a large part of the job. Brochures, fact sheets, pamphlets, and newsletters may be written for people visiting the park or nature center. Materials might also be sent to area residents in an effort to gain public support.

One aspect of protecting any natural area involves communicating facts and debunking myths about how to respect the area and the flora and fauna that inhabit it. Another aspect involves tending managed areas to promote a diversity of plants and animals. This may mean introducing trails and footpaths that provide easy yet noninvasive access for the public; it may mean cordoning off an area to prevent foot traffic from ruining a patch of rare moss; or it may mean instigating a letter-writing campaign to drum up support for legislation to protect a specific area, plant, or animal. It may be easy to get support for protecting the snowshoe rabbit; it is harder to make the public understand the need to preserve and maintain a bat cave.

Some naturalists, such as directors of nature centers or conservation organizations, have massive administrative responsibilities. They might recruit volunteers and supervise staff, organize long- and short-term program goals, and handle record keeping and the budget. To raise money, naturalists may need to speak publicly on a regular basis, write grant proposals, and organize and attend scheduled fund-raising activities and community meetings. Naturalists also try to increase public awareness and support by writing press releases and organizing public workshops, conferences, seminars, meetings, and hearings. In general, naturalists must be available as resources for educating and advising the community.

REQUIREMENTS
High School
If you are interested in this field, you should take a number of basic science courses, including biology, chemistry, and earth science. Botany courses and clubs are helpful, since they provide direct experience monitoring plant growth and health. Animal care experience, usually obtained through volunteer work, is also helpful. Take English courses in high school to improve your writing skills,

which you will use when writing grant proposals and conducting research.

Postsecondary Training

An undergraduate degree in environmental, physical, or natural sciences is generally the minimum educational requirement for becoming a naturalist. Common college majors are biology, forestry, wildlife management, natural resource and park management, natural resources, botany, zoology, chemistry, natural history, and environmental science. Course work in economics, history, anthropology, English, international studies, and communication arts is also helpful.

Graduate education is increasingly required for employment as a naturalist, particularly for upper-level positions. A master's degree in natural science or natural resources is the minimum requirement for supervisory or administrative roles in many of the nonprofit agencies, and several positions require either a doctorate or several years of experience in the field. For positions in agencies with international sites, work abroad is necessary and can be obtained through volunteer positions such as those with the Peace Corps or in paid positions assisting in site administration and management.

Other Requirements

If you are considering a career in this field, you should like working outdoors, as most naturalists spend the majority of their time outside in all kinds of weather. However, along with the desire to work in and with the natural world, you need to be capable of communicating with the human world as well. Excellent writing skills are helpful in preparing educational materials and grant proposals.

Seemingly unrelated skills, such as engine repair and basic carpentry, can be essential to managing a post. Because of the remote locations of many of the work sites, self-sufficiency in operating and maintaining equipment allows the staff to lose fewer days because of equipment breakdown.

EXPLORING

One of the best ways to learn about the job of a naturalist is to volunteer at one of the many national and state parks or nature centers. These institutions often recruit volunteers for outdoor work. College students, for example, are sometimes hired to work as summer or part-time nature guides. Outdoor recreation and training organizations, such as Outward Bound and the National Outdoor

Learn More About It

Baker, Nick. *Amateur Naturalist*. Washington, D.C.: National Geographic, 2005.

Botkin, Daniel B. *Strange Encounters: Adventures of a Renegade Naturalist*. New York: Tarcher, 2004.

Farber, Paul Lawrence. *Finding Order in Nature: The Naturalist Tradition from Linnaeus to E.O. Wilson*. Baltimore, Md.: Johns Hopkins University Press, 2000.

Huxley, Robert. *The Great Naturalists*. London, England: Thames & Hudson, 2007.

Montgomery, Sy. *The Curious Naturalist: Nature's Everyday Mysteries*. Camden, Me.: Down East Books, 2000.

Rinehart, Kurt. *Naturalist's Guide to Observing Nature*. Mechanicsburg, Penn.: Stackpole Books, 2006.

Wilson, Edward O. *Naturalist*. Washington, D.C.: Island Press, 2006.

Leadership School, are especially good resources. Most volunteer positions, though, require a high school diploma and some college credit.

You should also consider college internship programs. In addition, conservation programs and organizations throughout the country and the world offer opportunities for volunteer work in a wide variety of areas, including working with the public, giving lectures and guided tours, and working with others to build or maintain an ecosystem. For more frequent, up-to-date information, you can read newsletters, such as *Environmental Career Opportunities* (http://ecojobs.com), that post internship and job positions. The Web site EnvironmentalCareer.com (http://environmental-jobs.com) also offers job listings.

EMPLOYERS

Naturalists may be employed by state agencies such as departments of wildlife, fish and game, or natural resources. They may work at the federal level for the U.S. Fish and Wildlife Service or the National Park Service. Naturalists may also work in the private sector for such employers as nature centers, arboretums, and botanical gardens.

STARTING OUT

If you hope to become a park employee, the usual method of entry is through part-time or seasonal employment for the first several jobs, then a full-time position. Because it is difficult to get experience before completing a college degree, and because seasonal employment is common, you should prepare to seek supplemental income for your first few years in the field.

International experience with agencies that work beyond U.S. borders is helpful. This can be through the Peace Corps or other volunteer organizations that work with local populations on land and habitat management or restoration. Other volunteer experience is available through local restoration programs on sites in your area. Organizations such as the Nature Conservancy (http://nature.org), The Trust for Public Land (http://www.tpl.org), and many others buy land to restore, and these organizations rely extensively on volunteer labor for stewarding and working the land. Rescue and release centers work with injured and abandoned wildlife to rehabilitate them. Opportunities at these centers can include banding wild animals for tracking, working with injured or adolescent animals for release training, and adapting unreleasable animals to educational programs and presentations.

ADVANCEMENT

In some settings, such as small nature centers, there may be little room for advancement. In larger organizations, experience and additional education can lead to increased responsibility and pay. Among the higher-level positions is that of director, handling supervisory, administrative, and public relations tasks.

Advancement into upper-level management and supervisory positions usually requires a graduate degree, although people with a graduate degree and no work experience will still have to start in nearly entry-level positions. So you can either work for a few years and then return to school to get an advanced degree or complete your education and start in the same position as you would have without the degree. The advanced degree will allow you eventually to move further up in the organizational structure.

EARNINGS

Earnings for naturalists are influenced by several factors, including the naturalist's specific job (for example, a wildlife biologist, a water and soil conservationist, or a game manager), the employer (for example, a state or federal agency), and the naturalist's experience and education. The U.S. Fish and Wildlife Service reports that biologists working for this department have starting salaries at the GS-5 to GS-7 levels. In 2008 biologists at the GS-5 pay level earned annual salaries that ranged from $29,656 to $38,641, and those at the GS-7 level earned annual salaries that ranged from $33,057 to $42,290. The U.S. Fish and Wildlife Service further reports that biologists can expect to advance to as high as a GS-12 level, which in 2008 had an annual salary range of $54,367 to $70,844. In general, those working for state agencies have somewhat lower earnings, particularly at the entry level. And, again, the specific job a naturalist performs affects earnings. For example, the U.S. Department of Labor reports that conservation scientists had a median annual salary of $58,720 in 2008. However, some conservation workers put in 40-hour workweeks and make less than $20,000 annually. As with other fields, management positions are among the highest paying. Candidates who meet the qualifications for management positions usually have a bachelor's degree in wildlife management or other related fields and at least two or more years of experience in wildlife resources work.

For some positions, housing and vehicles may be provided. Other benefits, depending on employer, may include health insurance, vacation time, and retirement plans.

WORK ENVIRONMENT

Field naturalists spend a majority of their working hours outdoors. Depending on the location, the naturalist must work in a wide variety of weather conditions, from frigid cold to sweltering heat to torrential rain. Remote sites are common, and long periods of working either in isolation or in small teams is not uncommon for field research and management. Heavy lifting, hauling, working with machinery and hand tools, digging, planting, harvesting, and tracking may fall to the naturalist working in the field. One wildlife manager in Montana spent every daylight hour for several days in a row literally running up and down snow-covered mountains, attempting to tranquilize and collar a mountain lion. Clearly, this can be a physically demanding job.

Indoor work includes scheduling, planning, and classroom teaching. Data gathering and maintaining logs and records are required for many jobs. Naturalists may need to attend and speak at local community meetings. They may have to read detailed legislative bills to analyze the impact of legislation before it becomes law.

Those in supervisory positions, such as directors, are often so busy with administrative and organizational tasks that they may spend little of their workday outdoors. Work that includes guided tours and walks through nature areas is frequently seasonal and usually dependent on daily visitors.

Full-time naturalists usually work about 35 to 40 hours per week. Overtime is often required, and for those naturalists working in areas visited by campers, camping season is extremely busy and can require much overtime. Wildlife and range managers may be on call during storms and severe weather. Seasonal work, such as burn season for land managers and stewards, may require overtime and frequent weekend work.

Naturalists have special occupational hazards, such as working with helicopters, small airplanes, all-terrain vehicles, and other modes of transport through rugged landscapes and into remote regions. Adverse weather conditions and working in rough terrain make illness and injury more likely. Naturalists must be able to get along with the variety of people using the area and may encounter armed individuals who are poaching or otherwise violating the law.

Naturalists also have a number of unique benefits. Most prominent is the chance to live and work in some of the most beautiful places in the world. For many individuals, the lower salaries are offset by the recreational and lifestyle opportunities afforded by living and working in such scenic areas. In general, occupational stress is low, and most naturalists appreciate the opportunity to continually learn about and work to improve the environment.

OUTLOOK

While a growing public concern about environmental issues may cause an increased demand for naturalists, this trend could be offset by government cutbacks in funding for nature programs. Reduced government spending on education may indirectly affect the demand for naturalists, as school districts would have less money to spend on outdoor education and recreation. According to the U.S. Department of Labor, employment opportunities for all conservation scientists, including naturalists, are expected to grow more slowly than the average through 2016. Despite the limited number of available positions, the number of well-qualified applicants is expected to remain high.

FOR MORE INFORMATION

For information on environmental expeditions, contact

Earthwatch Institute
Three Clock Tower Place, Suite 100
PO Box 75
Maynard, MA 01754-2574
Tel: 800-776-0188
Email: info@earthwatch.org
http://www.earthwatch.org

For information about internships, career conferences, and publications, contact

Environmental Careers Organization
30 Winter Street, 6th Floor
Boston, MA 02108-4720
Tel: 480-515-2525
Email: admin@eco.org
http://www.eco.org

This group offers internships and fellowships for college and graduate students with an interest in environmental issues. For information, contact

Friends of the Earth
1717 Massachusetts Avenue, Suite 600
Washington, DC 20036-2002
Tel: 877-843-8687
http://www.foe.org

For information on a variety of conservation programs, contact

National Wildlife Federation
11100 Wildlife Center Drive
Reston, VA 20190-5362
Tel: 800-822-9919
http://www.nwf.org

For information on volunteer opportunities, contact

Student Conservation Association
PO Box 550
689 River Road
Charlestown, NH 03603-0550
Tel: 603-543-1700
http://www.thesca.org/

For information on federal employment, contact
USAJOBS
Office of Personnel Management
http://www.usajobs.opm.gov

For information on careers, contact
U.S. Fish and Wildlife Service
U.S. Department of the Interior
Division of Human Resources
4401 North Fairfax Drive, Mailstop: 2000
Arlington, VA 22203-1622
http://www.fws.gov/jobs/

Organic Farmers

OVERVIEW

Organic farmers manage farms that produce fruits, vegetables, herbs, dairy, or other products without the use of inorganic fertilizers and synthetic chemical herbicides, growth hormones, and synthetic pesticides. Depending on the size of the farm, organic farmers manage staff; handle crop production and schedules; work the land; operate and maintain machinery, and repair farm structures; take care of administrative tasks such as bookkeeping, tax reporting, phone calls, and emails; and market and promote the farm business.

HISTORY

Organic farming is an ancient practice, dating back to early civilizations, and was the only form of agriculture for thousands of years. Its distinction as "organic" was not needed, nor made, until the early 20th century, when another type of agricultural practice emerged that relied on synthetic fertilizers and chemicals to improve and increase crop productions. Sir Albert Howard, a British agriculturist, is considered by many to be the father of organic farming. He studied agricultural practices in India from 1905 to 1934, and later wrote books, such as *An Agricultural Testament,* about composting and soil fertility, recycling organic waste materials for use in farming, and his adamant opposition to the use of chemical fertilizers in farming.

Chemicals that were developed for use in World War II were adapted, post-war, for use in crop production in the United States; for instance, nerve gases were used as strong pesticides. To combat mosquitoes and other pests, these chemicals were used widely on crops around the country. It wasn't until 1962, when ecologist Rachel Carson's book *Silent Spring* came out, that the general public became fully aware of what these chemicals were doing to the environment, to wildlife and ecosystems, and to human beings. From the book, people learned that DDT (Dichlorodiphenyltrichloroethane), a colorless, chlorine-containing pesticide, was killing a number of different bird species (thus the book's title, silent spring), and that pesticides stay in people's systems their entire lives. Carson advocated for more responsible use of the chemicals, and for agricultural and chemical companies to be forthcoming about the use of these chemicals. DDT was banned in 1972, and *Silent Spring* is credited for kicking off the environmental movement.

Organic farming has evolved since the 1970s to take many forms. In the early days, many organic farmers started their businesses to directly counter large, industrialized farms. The small, independently operated organic farm still exists today, as do large, corporate farms. The term *organic* has evolved and been popularized, with people now interpreting it to mean anything from "free of chemicals" to "USDA organic certified." With "organic" becoming more closely associated with a corporate logo and large agribusiness, many small- and medium-sized organic farms are instead using the words "sustainable" and "natural" to describe their farming practices.

Organic farmer Keith Stewart describes sustainability as "having more small farms and few big ones, more farms run by individuals, families, and partnerships, and fewer farms run by publicly held corporations. Every farm, like every family, is unique. The small farmer who lives on his or her land will learn over time what is best for it. Sustainability is about having more food produced and consumed locally, or at least regionally. When a farm is part of a community, be it an organic farm or otherwise, it belongs, in a sense, not just to the farmer, but to the community as a whole. It enriches the community by providing open space, wildlife habitat, and scenic views. And it keeps alive a connection to one of the most elemental of human activities—the cultivation of food."

THE JOB

The International Federation of Organic Agriculture Movements defines organic farming as "a production system that sustains the health of soils, ecosystems, and people. It relies on ecological processes, biodiversity, and cycles adapted to local conditions, rather than the use of inputs with adverse effects. Organic agriculture combines tradition, innovation, and science to benefit the shared environment and promote fair relationships and a good quality of life for all involved."

Organic farmers either own the organic farmland on which they work, rent the land from the owner, or lease it through a land trust. Organic farmers may therefore be the farmland and business owners, *farm operators*, or they may be *farm managers*. They may come from a long line of farmers or they may be new to the business. On small farms, organic farmers have fewer staff and more diverse, wide-ranging responsibilities. They may be involved in more of the physical labor in addition to hiring and managing staff; researching, purchasing, and maintaining farm equipment; and researching and strategizing the types of crops to grow, the types of seeds to plant, and the timing of plantings and harvestings.

Some organic farmers change careers to become farmers, such as Keith Stewart. He was 40 when, in 1986, he traded in a well-established career as a project manager (and a tiny apartment) in New York City, for an "unkempt but fully functional dairy farm" 70 miles north of the city, in Westtown, New York. The 88-acre site, known as Keith's Farm, that he and his then-girlfriend, now-wife Flavia Bacarella purchased, includes an old house and a barn, "woods and fields, ridges and vales, a pond and a stream," as well as chickens, dogs, cats, and plenty of wildlife. The organic farm started as a one-person operation and has since grown to include a rotating staff of six to eight workers per year. And while the work of being a farmer has been, and continues to be, hard, Keith still believes the challenges are well worth the toil. "There has been much to learn," he says. "But when your heart agrees with what you are doing, the learning is easier and more fun. I've done many other kinds of work in my life, but none where I felt as appreciated or needed." Keith's Farm has developed a loyal clientele since it first broke ground and is the "longest-standing purveyor" at the Union Square Greenmarket in New York City.

A big part of organic farming involves soil management through crop rotation (also known as crop sequencing). To keep the soil fertile and help control pests and diseases, organic farmers will use the same farmland to plant a different crop in a schedule of either successive seasons or every few years. Composting is also part of the job description. Compost, or "green manure," is a natural fertilizer that can be created by mixing such things as decaying vegetables and food wastes, paper and yard wastes (such as grass clippings),

An organic farmer checks her crop of strawberries before harvesting them for sale at farmers' markets, specialty food stores, and restaurants. *AP Photo/Rita Beamish*

and animal waste (manure). Granted, it's not a pretty smell, but the combination is rich in minerals that help fertilize and condition the soil.

Depending on the size of the farm, organic farmers are responsible for preparing the land, mechanical tilling, weeding (by hand, tools, and devices such as the flame-weeder, which literally shoots flame to burn weeds), mulching, planting, fertilizing (composting), cultivating, and harvesting, and this is by no means an all-inclusive list. Work hours are especially long during planting, growing, and harvesting seasons. Once the harvest is over, they make sure that the produce is properly packaged, stored, and marketed. Many farmers participate in farmers' markets, and while this boosts sales, it also adds to the farmers' workload. It requires creating the vending booth (such as signage, product packaging, literature for takeaways, etc.); packing up and trucking the products to the market; setting up the booth; and either working at the market and interacting with consumers and handling transactions, or staffing the booth and managing the staffing schedules. And at the end of marketing day, every task needs to be reversed: The booth needs to be broken down, products must be packed up and brought back to the farm, and then the tallying and bookkeeping of the transactions can begin.

During cold seasons, farmers may plant cover crops, which are crops that are planted primarily to provide ground cover, prevent erosion, and improve soil properties. Cover crops may be wheat, oats, or rye, or can even be legumes, such as clover and alfalfa.

Organic farmers might also produce products such as milk, cheese, yogurt, and eggs. All organic dairy products and eggs must come from animals that are fed organic feed and are provided with access to open space where they can comfortably roam and enjoy the sunlight. Organic livestock and poultry may not be given antibiotics, hormones, or medications, but they may be vaccinated against disease.

REQUIREMENTS
High School
While in high school, take classes in business, math, earth science, ecology, agriculture (if offered), biology, English, and computers. Foreign language classes can also be useful.

Postsecondary Training
Self-employed farmers may have received their training while on the job, either from growing up in a farm family, or through adult

Community-Supported Agriculture

Community-Supported Agriculture (CSA) means the community helps support the farm. People can be "members" or "shareholders" of the farm by buying a "share." The share is actually a certain amount of produce from the farm that the shareholder gets on a regular basis, as the season permits. The farm will deliver the shareholders' share (vegetables, fruits, herbs, etc.) each week to a participating community center near where the shareholder lives. And then it's up to the shareholder to pick up his or her package at the center. If a shareholder neglects to pick up that week's share, the food is usually donated to a shelter or food pantry.

Roxbury Farm is one example of a community-supported farm. Located in Kinderhook, New York, it is one of the largest CSAs in the country, and the first to have a community in New York City. The 225-acre farm grows vegetables and herbs, and raises grass-fed animals for over 1,000 members representing 1,050 families across four counties: Columbia County, the Capital Region, Westchester County, and Manhattan. CSA members can also get more involved in the farm, if they like, by picking produce themselves from the U-pick garden, and participating in farm workdays, potlucks, and other events. They also receive a newsletter with farm and produce updates, and recipes and cooking tips. Learn more at http://www.roxburyfarm.com.

on-the-job training and continuing education courses and programs in agriculture. Others may have an associate or bachelor's degree in agriculture, which is becoming more important in the business of operating a farm. Degrees can be in farm management or in business with a concentration in agriculture. According to the U.S. Department of Labor, all state universities have a land-grant college or university with a school of agriculture. Students pursuing an agriculture degree typically take classes in agronomy, dairy science, agricultural economics and business, horticulture, crop and fruit science, and animal science. They may also study technical aspects of crops, growing conditions, and plant diseases. If interested in organic dairy farming, course work may include the basics of veterinary science and animal husbandry (which is the care and breeding of farm animals). Other key courses include climate change, the impact of farming on the environment, economic policy (as it relates to farming and farmland), as well as business management and accounting. Computer classes are also relevant as more farming businesses are using computer software programs for record keeping and document production. Many farms offer internships and apprenticeships, in which students can train while on the job, and earn school credit and possibly a small stipend in exchange for their work.

Certification or Licensing

Since 2002 the U.S. Department of Agriculture National Organic Program (NOP) has regulated the standards for farms that want to sell organic products. Farms that produce less than $5,000 worth of organic products per year are not required by the USDA to be certified. To receive the organic certification and use the official "USDA Organic" label, at least 95 percent of the ingredients must be organic and meet the USDA standards for organic production and processes. For some farmers, especially those at beginning and small farms, the USDA certification process can be expensive, and financial assistance may be required. The certification process also requires evidence of an organic farming plan, paperwork to verify the plan, and a certain number of farm inspections. Third-party agents are hired to conduct the inspections of the farmer, the farm, the production process, as well as all who work on the farm.

Keith's Farm, for example, was originally certified by the Northeast Organic Farming Association of New York (NOFA-NY), at a time when it set its own rules and standards for organic farming certification. The organization has since changed its name to NOFA-NY Certified Organic LLC, and is now following USDA national standards for organic certification.

According to the Organic Farming Research Foundation, in 1994 there were approximately 2,500 to 3,000 certified organic farmers in the United States. As of 2007, the number had jumped to 13,000 certified organic farmers, and certified organic farmland could be found in all 50 states.

Other Requirements

Self-motivated, disciplined, detail-oriented, and patient are the all-important character traits needed in organic farming. The self-motivation and discipline are called upon on a daily basis, and are especially crucial to have in the beginning years of farming. Waiting for things to grow—both the produce and the business itself—is where patience comes into play. As organic farmer Keith Stewart puts it, "We see the fruits of our labor and the results of our neglect. We are on good terms with the natural world, or we should be, and we inhabit it in a practical, down-to-earth way."

A love of the land and strong desire to work with and get closer to nature are a given in this job. Attention to detail while simultaneously juggling multiple tasks is also important on many levels, from managing the crop production and the farm staff, to managing and promoting the business itself and the products. "Dawn to dusk" does not quite cover the hours required to complete the work; the time commitment goes far, far beyond this. Excellent hand-eye coordination is required, as is the ability to safely handle farm equipment one moment and manage farm animals the next. Physical fitness, stamina, and energy are required and tested constantly. The work is predominantly outdoors in any kind of weather—be it teeming rain, blazing sunshine, bone-shattering cold, or the three deadly H's (hazy, hot, and humid). A good attitude, strong constitution, and openness to continually learn are extremely helpful attributes to have in this job.

EXPLORING

Keep your eyes and ears open for the documentary film *The Greenhorns*, directed by Severine von Tscharner Fleming, of Smithereen Farm in Hudson River Valley, New York. The film features conversations with young farmers across the country—those who deliberately set out to become farmers, and those who "accidentally" fell into it. The film advocates for choosing agriculture as a career. You can learn more about *The Greenhorns* and find other resources, such as "The Greenhorns Guide for Beginning Farmers," by visiting the Web site (http://www.thegreenhorns.net).

Another excellent way to explore the field (without breaking a sweat) is by reading books such as Keith Stewart's *It's a Long Road to a Tomato: Tales of an Organic Farmer Who Quit the Big City for the (Not So) Simple Life* (New York: Marlowe & Company, 2006); and Peter V. Fossel's *Organic Farming: Everything You Need to Know* (Osceola, Wis.: Voyageur Press, 2007). The trade publication *Farmers' Market Today* is another useful resource that will keep you up to date on tips, trends, and resources for farmers.

EMPLOYERS

Nearly 1.3 million farmers, ranchers, and agricultural managers worked in the United States in 2006, according to the U.S.

Department of Labor. About 80 percent were self-employed farm-ers and ranchers, and the rest were agricultural managers. Most worked in the area of crop-production management, while others were responsible for managing livestock and dairy production. Some organic farmers work independently on small farms; others may work on large farms, and may oversee many farm workers and staff.

STARTING OUT

Volunteering or working part time on an organic farm is an excel-lent way to learn what it takes to succeed in and enjoy being an organic farmer. A willingness to relocate to have the farm experi-ence can also broaden the range of opportunities. For example, Qayyum Johnson had worked on a farm in California before mov-ing to New York to work on Keith's Farm. And Matt Ready, an intern with Keith's Farm since June 2009, found his internship through ATTRA, an organization that offers a national directory called "Sustainable Farming Internships and Apprenticeships." (You can find the directory at: http://attra.ncat.org/attra-pub/internships/.) Matt had been studying computer science and doing landscaping work in Indiana when he got the idea about working on a farm. He started exploring farms around the country, and his sister's recent move to New York City inspired him to look closer at farms in the New York area. The internship at Keith's Farm was posted in ATTRA's directory. Matt and Qayyum live and work on the farm, along with a small team of workers. Their tasks are var-ied, including helping with plantings, harvestings, and greenhouse work; pitching in at the greenmarket; and tending to the chickens (and the eggs).

The nonprofit organization Worldwide Opportunities in Organic Farming (WWOOF) lists farms around the world where volunteers are needed. Visit the USA site to learn more about opportunities within the states (http://www.wwoofusa.org/), or if you're more adventurous and able to travel and spend a summer, or longer, away from home, visit the WWOOF headquarters' site (http://www.wwoof.org/index.asp).

ADVANCEMENT

The path of advancement in the farming business depends on the farmer. For some, advancement can come in the form of expanding into different products (such as offering baked goods in addition to produce), or increasing the size of the farm and the crops, and adding more staff. Advancement can also include participating in more farmers' markets, or starting up a community-supported aspect of the farm. For other farmers, advancement may take a more meditative, educational path, one that might lead to writing books and articles, or teaching, lecturing, and mentoring young farmers and students. Some even start restaurants on or near the farm.

A Few Words to Inspire Future Farmers

"Cultivators of the earth are the most valuable citizens. They are the most vigorous, the most independent, the most virtuous, and they are tied to their country and wedded to its liberty and interests by the most lasting bands. As long, therefore, as they can find employment in this line, I would not convert them into mariners, artisans, or anything else." —*Thomas Jefferson*

"Let us never forget that the cultivation of the earth is the most important labor of man. When tillage begins, other arts follow. The farmers, therefore, are the founders of human civilization." —*Daniel Webster*

"It is vitally important that we can continue to say, with absolute conviction, that organic farming delivers the highest quality, best-tasting food, produced without artificial chemicals or genetic modification, and with respect for animal welfare and the environment, while helping to maintain the landscape and rural communities." —*Prince Charles of Wales*

"The more we pour the big machines, the fuel, the pesticides, the herbicides, the fertilizer and chemicals into farming, the more we knock out the mechanism that made it all work in the first place." —*David R. Brower*

"There are only three things that can kill a farmer: lightning, rolling over in a tractor, and old age." —*Bill Bryson*

EARNINGS

Annual salaries for organic farmers vary each year, depending on the quantity and quality of the farm's products and consumers' demands for those products. Small farms that are new may not see much, if any, profit the first few years of the business. And even farms that have been in business for many years, with a longstanding customer base, may see large profit one year and less profit the following year.

The U.S. Department of Labor reports that in 2008, farmers and ranchers earned median annual incomes of $33,550, with the bottom 10 percent bringing home $19,920 per year, and the top 10 percent earning $96,630 or more annually. According to the USDA, in 2007 established farms had annual household incomes in the $90,866 range. Beginning farmers had household incomes that were 4 percent lower than those of established farm households. (The USDA defines "beginning farm" as one that's been in operation for less than 10 years.) According to an article in the USDA's publication *Amber Waves*, farmers work well past retirement, and tend to have "several income sources, different savings habits, and more diverse financial portfolios, including more personal savings, than other U.S. households." Farmers often supplement their incomes by working in other jobs as well, which can include running a separate business, teaching, or writing.

WORK ENVIRONMENT

Farmers work from dawn to dusk, rain or shine, and will work even longer hours during plantings and harvestings. If they run a small farm with few staff members, more of the responsibilities will fall to them, making for longer days and little, if any, time off. Much of their day is spent outside working the land, but they also spend some time indoors addressing the administrative side of the business, which can include conducting Internet research and reviewing and paying bills, among other tasks. They may spend some time traveling to participate in farmers' markets, conferences, and workshops.

OUTLOOK

The industrialization of agriculture has enabled large-scale farming businesses to get more done with fewer workers. This coupled with a continuing population growth and consequential urban sprawl (the spread of development, such as houses and shopping centers, into nearby undeveloped land, often prime farmland)—plus surging costs of land, machinery, and other farming necessities—has caused the demise of many farms, and made it especially challenging for young and beginning farmers to start their farming business. Larger, better-funded, and more established farms have been able to withstand the pressures, as well as take advantage of government subsidies and payments, since these are typically based on the amount of acreage owned and the per-unit production.

While the U.S. Department of Labor forecasts a moderate decline in employment growth (by about 8 percent) of self-employed farmers and ranchers through 2016, farmers who run small- and medium-sized businesses in a specific niche can take heart that they will find more opportunities in the industry. Keith Stewart points out that there are "some impressively bright spots" amid the dark picture. "While many rural communities are in decline, paradoxically, in and around large urban areas there is a resurgence of interest in small farms and the fresh, wholesome food they provide." Organic farmers who cater to urban and sub-urban customers, particularly by participating in farmers' markets and community-supported programs and cooperatives, will find that they have more avenues in which to promote their farms and sell their products. To further bolster this, reports show that more farmers' markets are opening every year in cities and sub-urbs throughout the country. In 1994 there were 1,755 farmers' markets operating in the United States; by mid-2008 that number had grown to 4,685, according to the USDA's Agricultural Marketing Service.

FOR MORE INFORMATION

Learn more about sustainable food and farm systems, and steps being taken to protect land and keep it healthy by visiting

American Farmland Trust
1200 18th Street, NW, Suite 800
Washington, DC 20036-2524
Tel: 202-331-7300
Email: info@farmland.org
http://www.farmland.org

Learn more about organic and sustainable farming and the certification program at NOFA-NY's Web site.

Northeast Organic Farming Association of New York
(NOFA-NY)
PO Box 880
Cobleskill, NY 12043-0880
Tel: 607-652-6632
http://nofany.org

Find organic farming research and learn more about issues related to the industry by visiting
Organic Farming Research Foundation
PO Box 440
Santa Cruz, CA 95061-0440
Tel: 831-426-6606
http://ofrf.org

Find membership information, books, public policy updates, and other resources on the OTA's Web site.
Organic Trade Association (OTA)
PO Box 547
Greenfield, MA 01302-0547
Tel: 413-774-7511
Email: info@ota.com
http://www.ota.com

Find resources and events for small farms and beginning farmers by visiting
United States Department of Agriculture
National Institute of Food and Agriculture
1400 Independence Avenue, SW, Stop 2201
Washington, DC 20250-2201
Tel: 202-720-4423
http://www.csrees.usda.gov/familysmallfarms.cfm

This organization is "part of a worldwide effort to link volunteers with organic farmers, promote an educational exchange, and build a global community conscious of ecological farming practices." Visit the U.S. Web site to learn more about volunteer opportunities on organic farms located across the country.
Worldwide Opportunities on Organic Farms – USA
PO Box 1098
Philmont, NY 12565-8098

Tel: 831-425-3276
Email: info@wwoofusa.org
http://www.wwoofusa.org

Organic Food Distributors

QUICK FACTS

School Subjects
Earth science
English

Personal Skills
Business/management
Communication/ideas

Work Environment
Mostly indoors
One or more locations

Minimum Education Level
Bachelor's degree

Salary Range
$26,000 to $42,000 to
$106,040+

Certification or Licensing
Required

Outlook
About as fast as the average

OVERVIEW

Foods that are labeled "organic" meet the organic food standards set by the U.S. Department of Agriculture (USDA). These foods can include produce, grains, meat, dairy, eggs, and processed food products. To be organic, they must be produced without most synthetic fertilizers and pesticides, genetic engineering, growth hormones, irradiation, and antibiotics. *Organic food distributors* serve as the middleman between food manufacturers and food service operators. They coordinate the logistics of the transportation and distribution of organically grown foods. They may work for or run a small business, or they may be part of a large operation, with a national and/or international clientele.

HISTORY

Until the development and use of synthetic pesticides and fertilizers in the 1940s, all farming was organic, and it was the oldest form of agriculture on this planet. Chemicals that were developed for use in World War II evolved into technologies to enhance and increase agricultural production and crop yields. For example, ammonium nitrate that was used for munitions during the war became the basis for ammonium nitrate fertilizer for crops. And organophosphate nerve gas evolved into strong pesticides. Many attribute the founding of the organic movement, which started in the 1930s and has since continued, to Sir Albert Howard, a British agriculturist who taught and wrote books about recycling organic waste materials for use in farming, in addition to other theories about composting and soil fertility, and health and disease. Walter Northbourne, a peer of Sir Howard's, is purported to have been the first to coin the term *organic* in relation to farming. He defined the organic farm as a single, interactive, and living entity, one that is composed of interrelated parts which function together to create the whole.

Awareness of the impact of chemicals on the health of the environment and living creatures increased in the 1960s and 1970s. DDT (Dichlorodiphenyltrichloroethane), a colorless, chlorine-containing pesticide, was used during World War II to control mosquitoes from spreading malaria and other diseases; post-war, it was used widely throughout the United States as an insecticide for crops. In her book *Silent Spring* (1962), ecologist Rachel Carson enlightened people to the harm that indiscriminate spraying of DDT and other pesticides was causing to the environment, animals (birds in particular), and people. She pointed out that these chemicals remain in people's bodies throughout their entire lives, and advocated for more responsible use of the chemicals and clear, honest reporting of information about their use and effects by agricultural and chemical companies. The book caused great controversy at the time, and opened people's eyes to what they had unknowingly been exposed to. The first Earth Day, which started in April 1970 as a global grassroots demonstration, also shone a spotlight on environmental issues and continues to this day as an annual event.

Demand for organic food has grown in the decades since, from small, organic farms catering to local clients, to large operations reaching a more mainstream clientele across the country. In 1990 Congress mandated the creation of a National Organic Standards Board and passed the Organic Foods Production Act. In 2000 the USDA issued the National Organic Program regulations, in which rules are laid out regarding prohibited and allowed substances in organic food production and processing, and what is required for a food to be labeled as "organic."

Learn More About It

Carson, Rachel. *Silent Spring.* New York: Mariner Books, 2002.
Fromartz, Samuel. *Organic, Inc.: Natural Foods and How They Grew.* Fort Washington, Pa.: Harvest Books, 2007.
Howard, Sir Albert. *An Agricultural Testament.* Emmaus, Pa.: Rodale Press, 1979.
Howard, Sir Albert. *Farming and Gardening for Health or Disease.* London, England: Faber and Faber, 1949.
Northbourne, Walter. *Look to the Land.* Hillsdale, N.Y.: Sophia Perennis, 2005.
Rodale, James. *The Organic Front.* Emmaus, Pa.: Rodale Press, 1949.

THE JOB

Organic food distributors are responsible for the logistics of how organic food gets from the manufacturing facility to retailers. They coordinate shipping, import and export, and freight. They may own the distribution company or they may work in such roles as *manager, sales or account representative,* or *import coordinator,* to name a few.

Managers may oversee staff in the marketing and promotion, finance, or human resources department of the distribution company. They may manage the warehouse where the products are packaged and shipped to food service operators. Business development managers help create business plans and attract new customers. Their responsibilities tie in closely with those of sales and account representatives, who are given weekly, monthly, and/or quarterly sales targets to meet. Sales representatives promote products to customers, developing and building close relationships with food stores and retailers, handling sales transactions and coordinating business agreements. Sales and account representatives work closely with managers, on teams and independently. Some jobs require previous experience working with clients in specific regions. Managers and account and sales representatives have a good understanding of the USDA rules and regulations pertaining to organic food distribution, and keep up with market trends in order to better target organic products to customers.

Import coordinators liaise between manufacturers and buyers, and coordinate with various departments within the food company. One recent posting for an import coordinator describes the job responsibilities as follows: assisting procurement personnel with purchase order entries; handling phone calls from growers; projecting products; answering sales phone lines; promoting customer service through phone conversations and email exchanges; handling buyer duties when needed; handling logistics regarding trucks and shipping, making sure deliveries reach company facilities on schedule; and ensuring growers' quality reports are filled out accurately. This job also requires fluency in English and Spanish, and the ability to travel when needed—locally and internationally, so a valid passport is needed—to visit growers and attend trade shows.

A good example of a national wholesale distributor of organic and natural products is United Natural Food Incorporated (UNFI). This company provides its customers and suppliers with services in distribution, marketing and promotion, merchandising, category management, and store support. UNFI has 18 distribution centers across the country, and carries over 60,000 products and supplies over 17,000 national clients, including natural food store chains, independent natural products retailers, conventional supermarkets, and the food service industry. Divisions within UNFI include Natural and Organic Products, which features 13 distribution centers servicing U.S. and international clients with frozen, refrigerated, dry grocery, bulk, supplements, health and beauty, pet, and general merchandise. Another division is Organic Produce and Fresh Produce, which is called Albert's Organics. This division consists of five distribution centers, servicing major metropolitan areas with an assortment of natural and organic produce, meat, dairy, and other fresh products.

Other departments in which people can work for organic food distributors include advertising, business analysis, customer service, drivers, information technology, marketing, operations, and purchasing.

REQUIREMENTS
High School
Course work in business, math, science, and English will provide a good basis for this field. Take agriculture, ecology, and environmental classes if your school offers them. Take foreign language classes (particularly Spanish) as well, as fluency in another language may be required for some organic food distribution jobs.

Postsecondary Training

While not required for some positions, a bachelor's degree enhances prospects for employment in the organic food industry. Take course work in business administration and management, economics, sales, communications, English, and computer programs. A master's in business administration is usually required of managers.

Certification or Licensing

Certification is voluntary and shows employers that you have achieved a level of skill and professionalism in your work. Sales representatives who complete formal training and pass an examination by the Manufacturers' Representatives Educational Research Foundation can secure the title of Certified Professional Manufacturers' Representative (CPMR) or Certified Sales Professional (CSP).

Licensing requirements for food distributors vary by state. For instance, according to the Texas Department of State Health Services, "Firms that engage in any of the following activities are required to obtain a food distributor license, a warehouse operator license, or a food distributor registration: sell any type of food product to any entity other than the final consumer; hold food that will be sold or distributed either by that entity or another; sell bulk raw materials (flour, sugar, grains, etc.) to any entity other than the final consumer." To learn more about the requirements for food distributor licensing, visit the Web site of the Department of Health in your state.

Other Requirements

Strong verbal and written communication skills are essential for most positions within the organic food distribution industry. Those working in sales, business development, marketing, and promotion, in particular, need solid organizational skills, the ability to work with and manage staff and clients, and knowledge of computer programs such as MS Excel, Outlook, Word, and PowerPoint. Enthusiasm, persistence, and creative problem-solving abilities are helpful. Familiarity with organic foods is important as well. Some jobs will require previous experience in and strong knowledge of one particular food if the distribution company only deals with one product. A valid driver's license is required for most sales and account representative jobs, and, as expected, for all drivers' jobs.

Certifiably Organic

The USDA gives meat and milk the certified organic label if the animals it comes from have never been fed, watered, or treated with pesticides, herbicides, antibiotics, or hormones. The animals must have access to pastures (not feedlots), where they get exercise and sunlight. Their feed must be certified organic as well, with no genetic modifications or animal byproducts. For produce to be certified organic, it must be grown on a farm that, for a minimum of three years, did not use synthetic fertilizers, herbicides, or pesticides or fertilizers and has not planted any genetically modified seeds, used fertilizers derived from sewage sludge, or treated seeds with irradiation.

EXPLORING

You can get a better idea of the types of jobs available in the organic food distribution industry by visiting such employment Web sites as Blue Sky Search (http://www.blueskysearch.com), which specializes in the produce, agriculture, and food industries, and Food Management Search (http://www.foodmanagementsearch.com). You can also visit the Web site of United Natural Foods Incorporated to gain a better understanding of the scope of work involved in organic food distribution (http://www.unfi.com).

EMPLOYERS

About 94,430 wholesale and manufacturing representatives worked for grocery and related wholesaler companies in 2006, according to the U.S. Department of Labor. Manufacturers and wholesale representatives held about 2 million jobs in the United States in 2006. Of these, nearly 60 percent worked in wholesale trade. Others were employed in manufacturing, retail trade, information, and construction. They either worked directly for firms or were self-employment agents for manufacturers.

STARTING OUT

Naturally, one of the best ways to get started in this career is to work for an organic food distributor or manufacturer. Use the Web to search for companies and job openings that interest you. Another way to get familiar with organic foods and test the waters is to work for an organic food retailer, such as Trader Joe's and Whole Foods. Read consumer and trade magazines and books to keep up with organic food business trends, and policies and regulations. And visit the Alternative Farming Systems Information Center on the USDA's Web site to learn more about organic food production and processes (http://afsic.nal.usda.gov).

ADVANCEMENT

Advancement in the organic food distribution field varies depending upon the job. Managers can move up to positions of higher authority in which they are responsible for overseeing more staff, coordinating more projects, and managing other regions. Sales or account representatives and import coordinators can also advance to management positions, overseeing staff and handling more clients. Advancement can also take the form of pursuing a master's or Ph.D. Those with years of experience and proven track records can start their own distribution companies or work as consultants within the industry.

EARNINGS

Wholesale and manufacturing representatives in general earned salaries ranging from $26,950 to $106,040 or higher in 2008, according to the U.S. Department of Labor.

In 2009 the median annual income for organic food distributors ranged from $26,000 to $42,000, depending on geographical location, according to findings on the salary Web site Indeed. com. To give some examples: Distributors in Hawaii, Maine, and Wisconsin took home salaries ranging from $26,000 to $28,000 per year; those in Arizona, California, Florida, Iowa, Indiana, and Michigan averaged between $31,000 and $36,000 per year; New Jersey and New York organic food distributors brought home the highest annual wages in 2009, earning $39,000 and $42,000 per year, respectively.

WORK ENVIRONMENT

Organic food distribution jobs usually require at least 40-hour workweeks. Work is indoors in offices, in manufacturing facilities and warehouses, and in cars and trucks, depending on the nature of the job. Managers and sales representatives may work longer hours and travel to cover different territories. Some jobs will require international travel as well, and therefore a valid passport will be required. Hours will vary, particularly if dealing with international customers, where adjustments to schedules are needed to be able to communicate with customers during their country's business hours. Drivers and warehouse workers may work morning, evening, or weekend shifts, depending on the company and delivery schedules.

OUTLOOK

Organic foods are still considered discretionary items by many people, meaning they are not necessities and people buy them when they choose to (as in, at their own discretion). While it is true that more people are concerned with living healthier lifestyles, the economy drives shoppers' decisions. For example, during a stable economy, consumers focus more on the quality of the products and less on the prices. During economic slowdowns and recessions, people pay more attention to their wallets and shop based on sales.

On the positive side, the USDA's Economic Research Service says, "Organic farming is becoming one of the fastest-growing segments of U.S. agriculture." Many food producers, manufacturers, distributors, and retailers are specializing in growing, processing, and marketing a widening array of organic foods. The Bureau of Labor Statistics does not forecast for organic food distributors specifically, but predicts that employment growth for wholesale and manufacturing representatives, in general, will be about as fast as the average for all occupations through 2016. Small, independent wholesale and manufacturing companies may be in greater need of independent agents and consultants in the coming years to help them market products to a wider customer base while controlling costs at the same time. Distributors with strong management and organizational skills and solid knowledge of the organic foods industry will have better odds of securing work.

FOR MORE INFORMATION

For more information about education, certification, and careers in manufacturing and distribution, visit the Web sites of these associations:

American Wholesale Marketers Association
2750 Prosperity Avenue, Suite 530
Fairfax, VA 22031-4338
Tel: 703-208-3358

Email: info@awmanet.org
http://www.awmanet.org

Manufacturers' Agents National Association
16 A Journey, Suite 200
Aliso Viejo, CA 92656-3317
Tel: 877-626-2776
Email: mana@manaonline.org
http://www.manaonline.org

**Manufacturers' Representatives Educational Research
  Foundation**
8329 Cole Street
Arvada, CO 80005-5834
Tel: 303-463-1801
http://www.mrerf.org

*To learn more about economic and policy issues regarding food, farming,
natural resources, and rural development, visit the USDA Economic
Research Service's Web site.*

United States Department of Agriculture
Economic Research Service
1800 M Street, NW
Washington, DC 20036-5831
http://www.ers.usda.gov

Range Managers

OVERVIEW

Range managers work to maintain and improve grazing lands on public and private property. They research, develop, and carry out methods to improve and increase the production of forage plants, livestock, and wildlife without damaging the environment; develop and carry out plans for water facilities, erosion control, and soil treatments; restore rangelands that have been damaged by fire, pests, and undesirable plants; and manage the upkeep of range improvements, such as fences, corrals, and reservoirs.

HISTORY

Early in history, primitive peoples grazed their livestock wherever forage was plentiful. As the supply of grass and shrubs became depleted, they simply moved on, leaving the stripped land to suffer the effects of soil erosion. When civilization grew and the nomadic tribes began to establish settlements, people began to recognize the need for conservation and developed simple methods of land terracing, irrigation, and the rotation of grazing lands.

Much the same thing happened in the United States. The rapid expansion across the continent in the 19th century was accompanied

What Is a Range?

The Society for Range Management defines Rangeland and Range Resources as follows: "Rangelands, a broad category of land comprising more than 40 percent of the earth's land area, are characterized by native plant communities, which are often associated with grazing, and are managed by ecological, rather than agronomic, methods."

The term *range* can also include forestlands that have grazing resources, or seeded lands that are managed like rangeland. Range resources are not limited to the grazeable forage, but may include wildlife, water, and many other benefits.

Source: http://www.rangelands.org

by destruction of plant and animal life and abuse of the soil. Because the country's natural resources appeared inexhaustible, the cries of alarm that came from a few concerned conservationists went unheeded. It was not until after 1890 that conservation became a national policy. Today several state and federal agencies are actively involved in protecting the nation's soil, water, forests, and wildlife.

Rangelands cover more than a billion acres of the United States, mostly in the western states and Alaska. Many natural resources are found there: grass and shrubs for animal grazing, wildlife habitats, water from vast watersheds, recreation facilities, and valuable mineral and energy resources. In addition, scientists use rangelands to conduct studies of the environment.

THE JOB

Range managers are sometimes known as *range scientists, range ecologists,* or *range conservationists.* Their goal is to maximize range resources without damaging the environment. They accomplish this in a number of ways.

To help ranchers attain optimum production of livestock, range managers study the rangelands to determine the number and kind of livestock that can be most profitably grazed, the grazing system to use, and the best seasons for grazing. The system they recommend must be designed to conserve the soil and vegetation for other uses, such as wildlife habitats, outdoor recreation, and timber.

Grazing lands must continually be restored and improved. Range managers study plants to determine which varieties are best suited to a particular range and to develop improved methods for reseeding. They devise biological, chemical, or mechanical ways of controlling undesirable and poisonous plants, and they design methods of protecting the range from grazing damage.

Range managers also develop and help carry out plans for water facilities, structures for erosion control, and soil treatments. They are responsible for the construction and maintenance of such improvements as fencing, corrals, and reservoirs for stock watering.

Although a great deal of range managers' time is spent outdoors, they also spend some time in offices, consulting with other conservation specialists, preparing written reports, and doing administrative work.

Rangelands have more than one use, so range managers often work in such closely related fields as wildlife and watershed management, forest management, and recreation. Soil conservationists and naturalists are concerned with maintaining ecological balance both on the range and in the forest preserves.

REQUIREMENTS
High School
If you are interested in pursuing a career in range management, you should begin planning your education early. Since you will need a college degree for this work, take college preparatory classes in high school. Your class schedule should include the sciences, such as earth science, biology, chemistry, and zoology (if your school offers it). Take mathematics and economics classes. Any courses that teach you to work with a computer will also be beneficial. You will frequently use this tool in your career to keep records, file reports, and do planning. English courses will also help you develop your research, writing, and reading skills. You will need all of these skills in college and beyond.

Postsecondary Training
The minimum educational requirement for range managers is usually a bachelor's degree in range management or range science. To be hired by the federal government, you will need at least 42 credit hours in plant, animal, or soil sciences and natural resources management courses, including at least 18 hours in range management.

If you would like a teaching or research position, you will need a graduate degree in range management. Advanced degrees may also prove helpful for advancement in other jobs.

To receive a bachelor's degree in range management, students must have acquired a basic knowledge of biology, chemistry, physics, mathematics, and communication skills. Specialized courses in range management combine plant, animal, and soil sciences with the principles of ecology and resource management. Students are also encouraged to take electives, such as economics, forestry, hydrology, agronomy, wildlife, and computer science.

While a number of schools offer some courses related to range management, only nine colleges and universities have degree programs in range management or range science that are accredited by the Society for Range Management. More than 40 other schools offer course work available in a discipline with a range management or range science option.

Certification or Licensing

The Society for Range Management offers certification as a certified range management consultant (CRMC) or a certified professional in rangeland management (CPRM). These are voluntary certifications, but they demonstrate a professional's commitment to the field and the high quality of his or her work. Requirements for certification include having a bachelor's degree and at least five years of experience in the field as well as passing a written exam.

Other Requirements

Along with their technical skills, range managers must be able to speak and write effectively and to work well with others. Range managers need to be self-motivated and flexible. They are generally persons who do not want the restrictions of an office setting and a rigid schedule. They should have a love for the outdoors as well as good health and physical stamina for the strenuous activity that this occupation requires.

EXPLORING

As a high school student, you can test your appetite for outdoor work by applying for summer jobs on ranches or farms. Other ways of exploring this occupation include a field trip to a ranch or interviews with or lectures given by range managers, ranchers, or conservationists. Any volunteer work with conservation organizations—large or small—will give you an idea of what range managers do and will help you when you apply to colleges and for employment.

As a college student, you can get more direct experience by applying for summer jobs in range management with such federal agencies as the Forest Service, the Natural Resources Conservation Service (NRCS), and the Bureau of Land Management (BLM). This experience may better qualify you for jobs when you graduate.

EMPLOYERS

Most range managers work for the federal government in the BLM or the NRCS. State governments employ range managers in game and fish departments, state land agencies, and extension services.

In private industry, the number of range managers is increasing. They work for coal and oil companies to help reclaim mined areas, for banks and real estate firms to help increase the revenue from landholdings, and for private consulting firms and large ranches. Some range managers with advanced degrees teach and do research at colleges and universities. Others work overseas with U.S. and UN agencies and with foreign governments.

STARTING OUT

The usual way to enter this occupation is to apply directly to the appropriate government agencies. People interested in working for the federal government may contact the Department of Agriculture's Forest Service, the NRCS, the Department of the Interior's Bureau of Indian Affairs, or the BLM. Others may apply to local state employment offices for jobs in state land agencies, game and fish departments, or agricultural extension services. Your college career services office should have listings of available jobs, and you can also conduct your own job search through the Internet.

ADVANCEMENT

Range managers may advance to administrative positions in which they plan and supervise the work of others and write reports. Others may go into teaching or research. An advanced degree is often necessary for the higher-level jobs in this field. Another way for range managers to advance is to enter business for themselves as range management consultants or ranchers.

EARNINGS

According to the U.S. Department of Labor, in 2008 foresters had annual incomes ranging from $34,710 to $78,350, depending on their years of experience and type of employer. The median salary for foresters in 2008 was $53,750. Those that worked for state governments averaged $48,930 per year, while federally employed foresters took home $60,670 per year. Conservations scientists' annual salaries are slightly higher by comparison. In 2008 their average annual income was $58,720, with the bottom 10 percent earning $35,190 and the top 10 percent averaging $86,910 or more per year.

Private companies pay their range managers salaries that are about the same as those paid by federal and state governments. Range managers are also eligible for paid vacations and sick days, health and life insurance, and other benefits.

WORK ENVIRONMENT

Range managers, particularly those just beginning their careers, spend a great deal of time on the range. That means they must work outdoors in all kinds of weather. They usually travel by car or small plane, but in rough country they use four-wheel-drive vehicles or get around on horseback or on foot. When riding the range, managers may spend a considerable amount of time away from home, and the work is often quite strenuous.

As range managers advance to administrative jobs, they spend more time working in offices, writing reports, and planning and supervising the work of others. Range managers may work alone or under direct supervision. They also often work as part of a team. They deal with people constantly—not only their superiors and coworkers, but also with the general public, ranchers, government officials, and other conservation specialists.

OUTLOOK

This is a small occupation, and most of the openings will arise when older, experienced range managers retire or leave the occupation. The U.S. Department of Labor predicts that job growth will be slower than the average through 2016 for conservation scientists and foresters, a category that includes range managers. The need for range managers should be stimulated by a growing demand for wildlife habitats, recreation, and water as well as by an increasing concern for the environment. A greater number of large ranches will employ range managers to improve range management practices and increase output and profitability. Range specialists will also be employed in larger numbers by private industry to reclaim lands damaged by oil and coal exploration. A small number of new jobs will result from the need for range and soil conservationists to provide technical assistance to owners of grazing land through the NRCS.

An additional demand for range managers could be created by the conversion of rangelands to other purposes, such as wildlife habitats and recreation. Federal employment for these activities, however, depends on the passage of legislation concerning the management of range resources, an area that is always controversial. Smaller budgets may also limit employment growth in this area.

FOR MORE INFORMATION

Career and education information may be obtained from

National Recreation and Park Association
22377 Belmont Ridge Road
Ashburn, VA 20148-4501
Tel: 800-626-6772
http://www.nrpa.org

This organization has career, education, scholarship, and certification information. Student membership is also available through its International Student Conclave.

Society for Range Management
10030 West 27th Avenue
Wheat Ridge, CO 80215-6601
Tel: 303-986-3309
Email: srmweb@rangelands.org
http://www.rangelands.org

For information about career opportunities in the federal government, contact these organizations:

U.S. Department of Agriculture
Natural Resources Conservation Service
PO Box 2890
Washington, DC 20013-2890
http://www.nrcs.usda.gov

U.S. Department of Agriculture
U.S. Forest Service
1400 Independence Avenue, SW
Washington, DC 20250-0003
Tel: 800-832-1355
http://www.fs.fed.us

U.S. Department of the Interior
Bureau of Indian Affairs
1849 C Street, NW
Washington, DC 20240-0001
Tel: 202-208-3710
http://www.doi.gov/bia

U.S. Department of the Interior
Bureau of Land Management
1849 C Street, NW, Room 5665
Washington, DC 20240-0001
Tel: 202-208-3801
http://www.blm.gov

U.S. Department of the Interior
National Park Service
1849 C Street, NW
Washington, DC 20240-0001
Tel: 202-208-5391
http://www.nps.gov

Recycling Coordinators

OVERVIEW

Recycling coordinators manage recycling programs for city, county, or state governments or large organizations, such as colleges or military bases. They work with waste haulers and material recovery facilities to arrange for collecting, sorting, and processing recyclables such as aluminum, glass, and paper from households and businesses. Recycling coordinators are often responsible for educating the public about the value of recycling as well as instructing residents on how to properly separate recyclables in their homes. Recycling coordinators keep records of recycling rates in their municipality and help set goals for diversion of recyclables from the waste stream.

HISTORY

Coordinating recycling as the job is known today has a brief history. Only in the 1980s and early 1990s did many states begin setting recycling goals, creating the need for recycling coordinators at the local level. Prior to that time, private citizen groups or industry led most recycling efforts, so there was little need for municipal recycling coordinators. While much of today's recycling is driven by a desire to improve the environment, earlier recycling was often driven by economic forces. During the Great Depression, individual citizens or groups, such as the Boy Scouts, held newspaper drives and turned the collected newspapers over to a recycler. The recycler paid a minimal amount for the collection of the newspapers and then generally sold the newspaper to industry, which recycled or otherwise reused the newspaper. During World War II, shortages in raw materials to support the war prompted citizens to hold drives for aluminum, rubber, paper, and scrap metal; this time the spirit of recycling was patriotic as well as economic.

Other than times of shortage, governments had little concern for how people disposed of waste, simply because there was relatively little waste. Municipalities had been dumping, burning, burying, or otherwise disposing of residents' waste for years with little consequence. In 1898 New York City opened the first garbage-sorting plant in the United States, recycling some of its trash. The first aluminum recycling plants were built in the early 1900s in Chicago and Cleveland. By the 1920s about 70 percent of U.S. cities had limited recycling programs, according to the League of Women Voters.

Can buybacks began in the 1950s; newspaper was first recycled in 1961 by a mill in New Jersey. By 1960 the United States recycled about 7 percent of its municipal waste. In the mid-1960s the federal government began to take greater interest in municipal waste-handling methods. Part of the Solid Waste Disposal Act of 1965 granted money for states to develop waste-handling programs. The Resource Conservation and Recovery Act of 1970, along with 1976 amendments to the act, defined types of municipal solid waste (MSW) and spelled out minimum standards for waste handling.

State and federal governments, such as branches of the Environmental Protection Agency, were the earliest to hire people who specialized in recycling. These recycling experts usually acted in an advisory capacity to local governments that were trying to develop their own programs.

In the 1990s more states began to set recycling goals, driving the increase in need for recycling coordinators. By 1998 all but six states had set formal recycling goals. These goals are generally stated in terms of the percentage of waste to be diverted from ending up in a landfill. Most states set goals between 20 and 50 percent. To encourage counties to make the effort at a local level, many state governments offered grants to counties to fund new recycling programs, and many counties found they needed a full-time worker to coordinate the new effort. Initially, only the most populous counties qualified for the grants to afford a recycling program because they could divert the highest volume from landfills.

THE JOB

As recycling becomes more widespread, fewer recycling coordinators are faced with the task of organizing a municipal program from scratch. Instead, recycling coordinators work to improve current recycling rates in several ways. While recycling coordinators spend some time on administrative tasks, such as meeting with waste haulers and government officials and writing reports, they often need a considerable amount of time for public-education efforts. One recycling coordinator in North Dakota notes that only a small portion of the average recycling coordinator's job is spent sitting behind a desk.

Educating the public on proper separation of recyclables and on the need for recycling is a large part of a recycling coordinator's job. Good oral communication skills are essential for a recycling coordinator to succeed in this role. Getting people who haven't recycled before to start doing so can take some convincing. Recycling coordinators spread their message by speaking to community groups, businesses, and schools. They use persuasive speaking skills to urge people to do the extra work of peeling labels from and washing bottles and jars instead of just throwing them out, and separating newspapers, magazines, cardboard, and other types of paper. Even as recycling increases in this country, many people are accustomed to disposing of trash as quickly as possible without giving it a second thought. It is the task of a recycling coordinator to get people to change such habits, and how well a recycling coordinator is able to do this can make the difference in the success of the entire program.

In some communities, recycling coordinators have economics on their side when it comes to getting people to change their habits. In so-called pay-as-you-throw programs, residents pay for garbage disposal based on how much waste their household produces. So recycling, although it may mean extra work, makes sense because it saves the homeowner money. For example, residents may be charged extra for any waste they set out at the curb beyond one garbage can per week. In communities with these programs, recycling rates tend to be higher, and recycling coordinators have an easier task of convincing people to recycle. Another part of a recycling coordinator's role as educator is answering questions about how recyclables are to be separated. Especially with new programs, residents often have questions about separating recyclables, such as what type of paper can be set out with newspaper, whether labels should be peeled from jars, and even keeping track of which week of the month or day of the week they should set their recyclables out with the trash. Fielding these types of calls always demands some portion of a recycling coordinator's time.

Most recycling coordinators spend a minimal amount of time on record keeping, perhaps 5 percent, one coordinator estimates. The coordinator is responsible for making monthly, or sometimes quarterly, reports to state and federal government agencies. Recycling coordinators also fill out grant applications for state and federal funding to improve their programs.

Some recycling coordinators work on military bases or college campuses. The goal of a recycling coordinator in one of these settings is the same as a municipal recycling coordinator—getting people to recycle. Their responsibilities may differ, however. The recycling coordinator on a college campus, for example, has a new set of residents every year to educate about the college's recycling program.

Recycling coordinators who come up with creative uses for waste may find opportunities in other fields as well. For example, recycling of computers and computer parts is a growing area. Some with knowledge in this area have founded their own companies or work for computer manufacturers.

REQUIREMENTS
High School
Recycling coordinators need a variety of skills, so taking a variety of classes in high school is a good start. Classes in business, economics, and civics are a good idea to help build an understanding of the public sector in which most recycling coordinators work. Knowledge of how local governments and markets for recycled materials function is something you will need to know later, and civics and economics courses provide this framework. English and speech classes are vital to developing good oral and written communication skills that you use to spread the word about the importance of recycling. Mathematics and science classes will prove useful in setting recycling goals and understanding how recycling helps the environment.

Postsecondary Training
Until recently, people with widely varying backgrounds and experience were becoming recycling coordinators. Enthusiasm, an

understanding of recycling issues, and business acumen were more important than any specific degree or professional background. This is still true to some extent, as colleges generally don't offer degrees in recycling coordination. Instead, a bachelor's degree in environmental studies or a related area and strong communication skills are desirable. Some schools offer minors in integrated waste management. Classes may include public policy, source reduction, transformation technology (composting/waste energy), and landfills, according to the Environmental Careers Organization (ECO).

Other Requirements
Useful personal skills include good communication and people skills for interacting with staff, contractors, government officials, and the public. Leadership, persuasiveness, and creativity (the ability to think of new ways to use collected materials, for example) also are important.

EXPLORING
You can start to explore a career as a recycling coordinator by familiarizing yourself with the issues involved in the field. Why is sorting garbage so costly? Why are some materials recycled and not others? Where are the markets? What are some creative uses for recyclable materials? Find out what's going on both nationally and in your area. Some states have more extensive recycling programs than others; for example, some have bottle deposit laws or other innovative programs to boost recycling efforts. Get to know who's doing what and what remains to be done. Read industry-related magazines; two informative publications are *Recycling Today* (http://www.recyclingtoday.com) and *Resource Recycling* (http://www.resource-recycling.com). A useful book that focuses on environmental career possibilities is *The Complete Guide to Environmental Careers in the 21st Century*, by the ECO.

Arrange a tour of a local material recovery facility and talk with the staff there. You might even volunteer to work for a recycling organization. Large and small communities often have groups that support recycling with fund drives and information campaigns. Also, most municipal public meetings and workshops are good places to learn about how you can help with recycling in your community.

EMPLOYERS

Recycling coordinators are almost exclusively employed by some level of government; they oversee recycling programs at the city, county, or state level. A limited number of recycling coordinators may find work with waste haulers that offer recycling coordination as part of their contracts to municipalities. Recycling coordinators work in communities of all sizes—from rural countywide programs to urban ones. When states first mandated recycling, larger counties that generated more waste generally were the first to hire recycling coordinators. However, as more states set and achieve higher recycling goals, smaller cities and even rural areas need someone to coordinate their growing programs. At the state level, state environmental protection agencies or community development agencies may employ coordinators to administer state grants to and advise local recycling programs all over the state. Large organizations, such as colleges or military bases, are other employers of recycling coordinators.

STARTING OUT

A first job as a recycling coordinator is most likely to be with a smaller municipal program. Most colleges have a network of career referral services for their graduates, and city or county governments with openings for recycling coordinators often use these services to advertise positions to qualified graduates. Positions at the state level also may be available. Someone with previous experience with waste management projects, issues, and operations, in addition to the right educational background, is likely to get the more sought-after positions in larger cities and state governments. Hands-on experience can be gained through internships, volunteering, cooperative education, summer employment, or research projects.

Volunteering or working at a part-time or summer job with a recycling program in your area is a great way to learn more about the job. Volunteering for a waste management consulting firm or nonprofit environmental organization is another way to get practical experience with recyclables.

ADVANCEMENT

In most cases, the position of recycling coordinator is the top spot in the recycling program. Advancement isn't really an option, unless

Don't Trash That TV!

Although technology has made many aspects of life more enjoyable and convenient, items such as personal computers, cell phones, and televisions become outdated almost as soon as you walk out of the store. It almost seems as if you can open the paper the next day and find a newer model with more features and an improved design. Since many consumers want the newest and most advanced technology available, and since old electronics tend to do little more than collect dust, there is an ever increasing amount of old electronic equipment showing up in today's garbage. A recent study estimates that nearly 500 million personal computers have become obsolete, and subsequently junked, in the United States since 1997. One problem with simply throwing these items out with your regular garbage is the possible contaminants they contain. For example, televisions and computer monitors contain cathode ray tubes (CRTs), which contain significant amounts of lead. Other electronic products contain nickel, cadmium, and other heavy metals that can be dangerous to humans and the environment.

Thus, the National Recycling Coalition recommends that you check with your state or local recycling board to see how to properly dispose of electronic equipment. Your town or county may even have regular pickup dates for such materials. You can also contact the manufacturer of your computer, television, or other electronic device to see if they offer recycling services or can put you in touch with a local organization that does.

As an alternative, and especially if the equipment still works, consider donating it to a charitable organization, small business, or local school that might have a need for it. For information on where you can donate computers, visit http://www.nrc-recycle.org/consumers.aspx. Taking the time to consider what to do with your obsolete electronics can make an important difference in the environment and in everyone's quality of life.

Source: The National Recycling Coalition's Electronic Recycling Initiative, http://www.nrc-recycle.org

the coordinator moves to another, perhaps larger, municipal program, to a private employer, or in some cases, to a different career field. There is a fair amount of turnover in the field because recycling coordinator positions, in many cases, are training ground for college graduates who eventually move on to other fields where they use skills they developed as recycling coordinators. Because recycling coordinators develop so many useful skills, they often find work in related fields, such as small business administration and nonprofit organizations or as government administrators.

Since many states have waste-handling projects, someone with good experience at the local level might move into a state-level job, such as recycling expert, a position in some states' waste-handling departments. Opportunities with private businesses that have in-house recycling needs or with solid-waste management consultants or businesses might also constitute advancement. Finally, recycling coordinators also have the opportunity to expand their own programs. Through their efforts, a modest program with a limited staff and budget could blossom into a full-scale, profitable venture for the community. The coordinator could conceivably extend the scope of the program; improve links with state or local government officials, the public, and private business and industry; receive more funding; add staff; and otherwise increase the extent and prominence of the program.

EARNINGS

The average annual salary for recycling coordinators was $37,000 in 2009, according to SimplyHired.com. Salaries vary by level of experience and type of company. For instance, an Internet posting for a recycling coordinator for a Maryland-based trucking and trash removal company listed the salary at $45,000 to $50,000. Another posting for a recycling program coordinator at the University of Washington offered a salary range between $32,400 and $43,200. Another thing to bear in mind is that positions in areas with a higher cost of living, such as California, Arizona, New York, and Washington, D.C., for example, tend to pay more.

According to the U.S. Department of Labor, median annual earnings of environmental engineers were $74,020 in 2008. Environmental engineering technicians had median annual earnings of $40,230 in 2008.

Benefits vary, but most local governments offer full-time employees a benefits package that generally includes paid health insurance; a retirement plan; and holiday, vacation, and sick pay.

WORK ENVIRONMENT

Recycling coordinators are essentially administrators. As such, they primarily work indoors, either in their offices or in meetings or giving speeches. Recycling coordinators need to watch costs, understand markets, and work within budgets. They should be able to be firm with contractors when necessary. They need to demonstrate good judgment and leadership, and they may need to justify their decisions and actions to city council members or others. Stresses are part of the job, including dealing with government bureaucracy, dips in community participation, services that fall short of expectations, fluctuating markets for recyclables, and other less-than-ideal situations.

Generally, recycling coordinators work 40 hours per week if they are full-time employees. Some positions may be part time, but for both work arrangements, working hours are generally during the day with weekends off. Occasionally, recycling coordinators may need to attend meetings in the evening, such as a county or city board meeting, or speak before a community group that meets at night. Facility or landfill tours that a recycling coordinator may arrange or participate in to generate publicity for the program may be offered on weekends. Recycling coordinators may leave the office setting to visit the material recovery facility, which can be noisy and dirty if compacting equipment and conveyers are running.

OUTLOOK

The outlook for municipal recycling coordinators is good. According to findings from the U.S. Recycling Economic Information Study, the recycling and reuse industry consists of approximately 56,000 establishments that employ over 1.1 million people, generate an annual payroll of nearly $37 billion, and gross over $236 billion in annual revenues. As states strive to meet their increasingly ambitious waste-reduction and recycling goals, people who can make it happen on the local level are going to be crucial. Although the recycling industry is subject to business fluctuations, demand and new technologies have created a viable market for recycled materials.

The recycling industry is also subject to political and social trends. Jobs will decline under administrations that do not allocate as much money for environmental concerns. On the other hand, more jobs may become available as engineers and technicians are attracted by the higher salaries offered in more popular technology- and finance-oriented fields. This environmental career, among others, is also starting to be recognized as its own field, and not just a subspecialty of other fields, such as civil engineering.

Nationwide, the waste management and recycling industries will be needing more people to run recovery facilities, design new recycling technologies, come up with new ways to use recyclables, and do related work. Private businesses are also expected to hire recycling coordinators to manage in-house programs.

FOR MORE INFORMATION

For up-to-date information on recycling, contact
American Forest and Paper Association
1111 19th Street, NW, Suite 800
Washington, DC 20036-3652
Tel: 800-878-8878
Email: info@afandpa.org
http://www.afandpa.org

For information on education and training, contact
Environmental Careers Organization
Tel: 480-515-2525
Email: admin@eco.org
http://www.eco.org

This organization provides technical information, education, training, outreach, and advocacy services.
National Recycling Coalition
805 15th Street, NW, Suite 425
Washington, DC 20005-2239
Tel: 202-789-1430
Email: info@nrc-recycle.org
http://www.nrc-recycle.org

For information on solid waste management, contact
National Solid Wastes Management Association
4301 Connecticut Avenue, NW, Suite 300
Washington, DC 20008-2304
Tel: 800-424-2869
http://www.nswma.org

Soil Conservationists and Technicians

QUICK FACTS

School Subjects
Agriculture
Biology
Earth science

Personal Skills
Helping/teaching
Technical/scientific

Work Environment
Indoors and outdoors
Primarily multiple locations

Minimum Education Level
Bachelor's degree

Salary Range
$35,190 to $58,720
to $86,910+
(Conservationists)
$22,540 to $32,000 to
$51,810 (Technicians)

Certification or Licensing
Voluntary

Outlook
More slowly than the average
(Conservationists)
Little or no change
(Technicians)

OVERVIEW

Soil conservationists develop conservation plans to help farmers and ranchers, developers, homeowners, and government officials best use their land while adhering to government conservation regulations. They suggest plans to conserve and reclaim soil, preserve or restore wetlands and other rare ecological areas, rotate crops for increased yields and soil conservation, reduce water pollution, and restore or increase wildlife populations. They assess land users' needs, costs, maintenance requirements, and the life expectancy of various conservation practices. They plan design specifications using survey and field information, technical guides, and engineering field manuals. Soil conservationists also give talks to various organizations to educate land users and the public about how to conserve and restore soil and water resources. Many of their recommendations are based on information provided to them by soil scientists.

Soil conservation technicians work more directly with land users by putting the ideas and plans of the conservationist into action. In their work they use basic engineering and surveying tools, instruments, and techniques. They perform engineering surveys and design and implement conservation practices like terraces and grassed waterways. Soil conservation technicians monitor projects during and after construction and periodically revisit the site to evaluate the practices and plans.

HISTORY

In 1908 President Theodore Roosevelt appointed a National Conservation Commission to oversee the proper conservation of the country's natural resources. As a result, many state and local conservation organizations were formed, and Americans began to take a serious interest in preserving their land's natural resources.

Despite this interest, however, conservation methods were not always understood or implemented. For example, farmers in the southern Great Plains, wanting to harvest a cash crop, planted many thousands of acres of wheat during the early decades of the 20th century. The crop was repeated year after year until the natural grasslands of the area were destroyed and the soil was depleted of nutrients. When the area experienced prolonged droughts combined with the naturally occurring high winds, devastating dust storms swept the land during the 1930s. Parts of Oklahoma, Texas, Kansas, New Mexico, and Colorado suffered from severe soil erosion that resulted in desert-like conditions, and this ruined area became known as the Dust Bowl.

As a result of what happened to the Dust Bowl, Congress established the Natural Resources Conservation Service of the U.S. Department of Agriculture in 1935. Because more than 800 million tons of topsoil had already been blown away by the winds over the plains, the job of reclaiming the land through wise conservation practices was not an easy one. In addition to the large areas of the Great Plains that had become desert land, there were other badly eroded lands throughout the country.

Fortunately, emergency planning came to the aid of the newly established conservation program. The Civilian Conservation Corps (CCC) was created to help alleviate unemployment during the Great Depression of the 1930s. The CCC established camps in rural areas and assigned people to aid in many different kinds of conservation. Soil conservationists directed those portions of the CCC program designed to halt the loss of topsoil by wind and water action.

Much progress has been made in the years since the Natural Resources Conservation Service was established. Wasted land has been reclaimed and further loss has been prevented. Land-grant colleges have initiated programs to help farmers understand the principles and procedures of soil conservation. The Cooperative Research, Education and Extension Service (within the Department of Agriculture) provides workers who are skilled in soil conservation to work with these programs.

Throughout the United States today there are several thousand federally appointed soil conservation districts. A worker employed by the government works in these districts to demonstrate soil conservation to farmers and agricultural businesses. There are usually one or more professional soil conservationists and one or more soil conservation technicians working in each district.

THE JOB

Soil sustains plant and animal life, influences water and air quality, and supports human health and habitation. Its quality has a major impact on ecological balance, biological diversity, air quality, water flow, and plant growth, including crops and forestation. Soil conservationists and technicians help scientists and engineers collect samples and data to determine soil quality, identify problems, and develop plans to better manage the land. They work with farmers, agricultural professionals, landowners, range managers, and public and private agencies to establish and maintain sound conservation practices.

A farmer or landowner contacts soil conservationists to help identify soil quality problems, improve soil quality, maintain it, or stop or reverse soil degradation. Conservationists visit the site to gather information, beginning with past and current uses of the soil and future plans for the site. They consult precipitation and soil maps and try to determine if the way land is being currently used is somehow degrading the soil quality. Conservationists consider irrigation practices, fertilizer use, and tillage (meaning land-cultivating or tilling) systems. At least a five- to 10-year history of land use is most helpful for working in this field.

Site observation reveals signs of soil quality problems. The farmer or landowner can point out areas of concern that occur regularly, such as wet spots, salt accumulation, rills and gullies or excessive runoff water that could indicate erosion, stunted plant growth, or low crop yield. Samples are taken from these areas and tested for such physical, chemical, and biological properties as soil fertility, soil structure, soil stability, water storage and availability, and nutrient retention. Conservationists also look at plant characteristics, such as rooting depth, which can indicate density or compaction of the soil.

Once all the data are gathered and samples tested, conservationists analyze the results. They look for patterns and trends. If necessary,

A field technician bottles a soil sample at a copper mine for uranium testing. *AP Photo/Debra Reid, File*

they take additional samples to verify discrepancies or confirm results. They prepare a report for the farmer or landowner.

A team of conservationists, engineers, scientists, and the landowners propose alternative solutions for soil problems. All the alternatives must be weighed carefully for their possible effects on ecological balance, natural resources, economic factors, and social or cultural factors. The landowner makes the final decision on which solutions to use and a plan is drafted.

After the plan is in place, soil conservationists and technicians continue to monitor and evaluate soil conditions, usually over a period of several years. Periodic soil sampling shows whether progress is occurring, and if not, changes can be made to the plan.

The following brief examples show how the process works. A farmer has a problem with crop disease. He sees that the yield is reduced and the health of plants is poor. Soil conservationists and technicians consider possible causes and test soil for pests, nutrient deficiencies, lack of biological diversity, saturated soil, and compacted layers. Depending on test results, conservationists might suggest a pest-management program, an improved drainage system, the use of animal manure, or crop rotation.

Another farmer notices the formation of rills and gullies on his land along with a thinning topsoil layer. Soil conservationists' research shows that the erosion is due to such factors as lack of cover, excessive tillage that moves soil down a slope, intensive crop rotation, and low organic matter. Suggested solutions include reducing tillage, using animal manure, planting cover crops or strip crops, and using windbreaks.

Conservationists and technicians who work for the Bureau of Land Management, which oversees hundreds of millions of acres of public domain land, help survey publicly owned areas and pinpoint land features to determine the best use of public lands. Soil conservation technicians in the Bureau of Reclamation assist civil, construction, materials, or general engineers. Their job is to oversee certain phases of such projects as the construction of dams and irrigation planning. The Bureau's ultimate goal is the control of water and soil resources for the benefit of farms, homes, and cities.

Other soil conservation technicians work as *range technicians*, who help determine the value of rangeland, its grazing capabilities, erosion hazards, and livestock potential. *Physical science technicians* gather data in the field; they study the physical characteristics of the soil, make routine chemical analyses, and set up and operate test apparatus. *Cartographic survey technicians* work with *cartographers* (mapmakers) to map or chart the earth or graphically represent geographical information, survey the public domain, set boundaries, pinpoint land features, and determine the most beneficial public use. *Engineering technicians* conduct field tests and oversee some phases of construction on dams and irrigation projects. They also measure acreage, place property boundaries, and define drainage areas on maps. *Surveying technicians* perform surveys for field measurement and mapping in order to plan for construction, to check the accuracy of dredging operations, or to provide reference points and lines for related work. They gather data for the design and construction of highways, dams, topographic maps, and nautical or aeronautical charts.

REQUIREMENTS
High School
While in high school, you should take at least one year each of algebra, geometry, and trigonometry. Take several years of English to develop your writing, research, and speaking skills as these are skills you will need when compiling reports and working with others. Science classes are also important, including earth science, biology, and chemistry. If your high school offers agriculture classes, be sure to take any relating to land use, crop production, and soils.

Postsecondary Training
Conservationists hold bachelor's degrees in areas such as general agriculture, range management, crop or soil science, forestry, and agricultural engineering. Teaching and research positions require further graduate-level education in a natural resources field. Though government jobs do not necessarily require a college degree (a combination of appropriate experience and education can serve as a substitute), a college education can make you more desirable for a position. Many employers prefer soil conservation technicians with a minimum of two years of specialized training or an associate's degrees in applied science or science-related technology

Typical beginning courses include applied mathematics, communication skills, basic soils, botany, chemistry, zoology, and introduction to range management. Advanced courses include American government, surveying, forestry, game management, soil and water conservation, economics, fish management, and conservation engineering.

Conservationists and technicians must have some practical experience in the use of soil conservation techniques before they enter the field. Many schools require students to work in the field during the school year or during summer vacation before they can be awarded their degree. Jobs are available in the federal park systems and with privately owned industries.

Certification or Licensing
No certification or license is required of soil conservationists and technicians; however, becoming certified can improve your skills and professional standing. The American Society of Agronomy offers voluntary certification in soil science.

Most government agencies require applicants to take a competitive examination for consideration.

Other Requirements
Soil conservationists and technicians must be able to apply practical as well as theoretical knowledge to their work. You must have a working knowledge of soil and water characteristics; be skilled in management of woodlands, wildlife areas, and recreation areas; and have knowledge of surveying instruments and practices, mapping, and the procedures used for interpreting aerial photographs.

Soil conservationists and technicians should also be able to write clear, concise reports to demonstrate and explain the results of tests, studies, and recommendations. A love for the outdoors and an appreciation for all natural resources are essential for success and personal fulfillment in this job.

EXPLORING
One of the best ways to become acquainted with soil conservation work and technology is through summer or part-time work on a farm or at a natural park. Other ways to explore this career include joining a local chapter of the 4-H Club or National FFA Organization (formerly Future Farmers of America). Science courses that include lab sections and mathematics courses focusing on practical problem solving will also help give you a feel for this kind of work.

EMPLOYERS
About 75 percent of all conservation workers are employed by local and federal government agencies. At the federal level, most soil conservationists and technicians work for the Natural Resources Conservation Service, the Bureau of Land Management, and the Bureau of Reclamation. Others work for agencies at the state and

county level. Soil conservationists and technicians also work for private agencies and firms such as banks and loan agencies, mining or steel companies, and public utilities. A small percentage of workers are self-employed consultants that advise private industry owners and government agencies.

STARTING OUT

Most students gain outside experience by working a summer or part-time job in their area of interest. You can get information on summer positions through your school's career services office. Often, contacts made on summer jobs lead to permanent employment after graduation.

Most soil conservationists and technicians find work with state, county, or federal agencies. Hiring procedures for these jobs vary according to the level of government in which the applicant is seeking work. In general, however, students begin the application procedure during the fourth semester of their program and take some form of competitive examination as part of the process. College-placement personnel can help students find out about the application procedures. Representatives of government agencies often visit college campuses to explain employment opportunities to students and sometimes to recruit for their agencies.

You can learn more about soil technician job descriptions and projects by searching job listings posted on employment Web sites such as Indeed.com (http://www.indeed.com) and Environmental Jobs.com (http://www.ecojobs.com). Just key in the words "soil conservationist" and "soil technician."

ADVANCEMENT

Soil conservationists and technicians usually start out with a local conservation district to gain experience and expertise before advancing to the state, regional, or national level.

In many cases, conservationists and technicians continue their education while working by taking evening courses at a local college or technical institute. Federal agencies that employ conservationists and technicians have a policy of promotion from within. Because of this policy, there is a continuing opportunity for such workers to advance through the ranks. The degree of advancement that all conservationists and technicians can expect in their working careers is determined by their aptitudes, abilities, and, of course, their desire to advance.

Workers seeking a more dramatic change can transfer their skills to related jobs outside the conservation industry, such as farming or land appraisal.

EARNINGS

The majority of soil conservationists and technicians work for the federal government, and their salaries are determined by their government service rating. In 2008 the average annual salary for science conservationists was $58,720, according to the *Occupational Outlook Handbook*. The bottom 10 percent had annual salaries of $35,190 or less, and the top 10 percent earned $86,910 or more per year. Those who worked for the federal government had annual incomes of about $69,090 in 2008. The average annual salary for forest and conservation technicians in 2008 was $32,000. The lowest paid 10 percent earned $22,540 or less, and the highest paid 10 percent earned $51,801 or more, per year.

The salaries of conservationists and technicians working for private firms or agencies are roughly comparable to those paid by the federal government. Earnings at the state and local levels vary depending on the region but are typically lower.

Government jobs and larger private industries offer comprehensive benefit packages that are usually more generous than those offered at smaller firms.

WORK ENVIRONMENT

Soil conservationists and technicians usually work 40 hours per week except in unusual or emergency situations. They have opportunities to travel, especially when they work for federal agencies.

Soil conservation is an outdoor job. Workers travel to work sites by car but must often walk great distances to an assigned area. Although they sometimes work from aerial photographs and other on-site pictures, they cannot work from pictures alone. They must visit the spot that presents the problem in order to make appropriate recommendations.

Although soil conservationists and technicians spend much of their working time outdoors, indoor work is also necessary when generating detailed reports of their work to agency offices.

As assistants to professionals, soil conservation technicians often assume the role of government public relations representatives when dealing with landowners and land managers. They must be able to explain the underlying principles of the structures that they design and the surveys that they perform.

To meet these and other requirements of the job, conservationists and technicians should be prepared to continue their education both formally and informally throughout their careers. They must stay aware of current periodicals and studies so that they can keep up-to-date in their areas of specialization.

Soil conservationists and technicians gain satisfaction from knowing that their work is vitally important to the nation's economy and environment. Without their expertise, large portions of land in the United States could become barren within a generation.

OUTLOOK

The U.S. Department of Labor predicts employment for conservation scientists (a category including soil conservationists) to grow slower than the average through 2016, mainly due to budget restrictions in this area. Soil conservation technicians can expect little to no change in employment opportunities through 2016.

Nevertheless, the need for government involvement in protecting natural resources should remain strong. More opportunities may be available with state and local government agencies, which are aware of needs in their areas. The vast majority of America's cropland has suffered from some sort of erosion, and only continued efforts by soil conservation professionals can prevent a dangerous depletion of our most valuable resource: fertile soil.

Some soil conservationists and technicians are employed as research and testing experts for public utility companies, banks and loan agencies, and mining or steel companies. At present, a relatively small number of soil conservation workers are employed by these firms or agencies. According to the U.S. Department of Labor, states designing initiatives to improve water resources by preventing pollution by agricultural producers and industrial plants will need soil and water experts. New jobs may also result from the need for range and soil conservationists to provide technical assistance to owners of grazing land through the Natural Resources Conservation Service.

FOR MORE INFORMATION

For information on soil conservation careers and certification, contact
American Society of Agronomy
677 South Segoe Road

Madison, WI 53711-1086
Tel: 608-273-8080
Email: headquarters@agronomy.org
http://www.agronomy.org

Contact NRCS for information on government soil conservation careers. The Web site has information on volunteer opportunities.

Natural Resources Conservation Service (NRCS)
U.S. Department of Agriculture
Attn: Conservation Communications Staff
PO Box 2890
Washington, DC 20013-2890
http://www.nrcs.usda.gov

For information on soil conservation, college student chapters, and publications, contact

Soil and Water Conservation Society
945 SW Ankeny Road
Ankeny, IA 50021-9723
Tel: 515-289-2331
http://www.swcs.org

Sustainability Professionals

QUICK FACTS

School Subjects
Business
English
Math
Science

Personal Skills
Communication/ideas
Helping/teaching
Technical/scientific

Work Environment
Indoors and outdoors
One or more locations

Minimum Education Level
Bachelor's degree

Salary Range
$37,430 to $78,940 to
$137,020+

Certification or Licensing
Voluntary

Outlook
About as fast as the
average

OVERVIEW

Sustainability professionals work for companies that run, and are aiming to run, green businesses. They work in countless areas. They may work as green builders and architects, marketing and promotion directors for green companies, environmental directors or program directors for sustainable institutes, or IT specialists for environmental foundations. They can be finance directors, project managers, accountants, development directors, intern coordinators, biologists, ecologists, engineers, foresters and forestry technicians, and the list goes on. Companies with the mission to reduce carbon emissions and greenhouse gases, cut down on waste by recycling and reusing materials, and operate more sustainably to improve the environment and communities hire sustainability professionals for help in each aspect of business.

HISTORY

The definition of sustainability was created in 1987 in the report "Our Common Future," which was written for the United Nations World Commission on Environment and Development. According to this paper, "Sustainable development is development that meets the needs of the present without compromising the ability of future generations to meet their own needs. It contains within it two key concepts: the concept of 'needs,' in particular the essential needs of the world's poor, to which overriding priority should be given; and the idea of limitations imposed by the state of technology and social organization on the environment's ability to meet present and future needs." The Dictionary of Sustainable Management, a project of the Presidio Graduate School, points out that this definition also aligns with a tenet of the Native American Iroquois Confederacy regarding the "seventh generation," in which chiefs are mandated to consider the impact their actions will have on their descendants seven generations into the future. (You may also be familiar with Seventh Generation as the brand name of a line of environmentally responsible products for homes.)

Sustainability arose from the growing awareness of environmental issues in the 1950s and 1960s. Many organizations and agencies—such as the U.S. Environmental Protection Agency, the Environmental Defense Fund, the Natural Resources Defense Council, and Worldwatch Institute, among others—were formed in the 1960s and 1970s to help publicize and address issues such as controlling pollution, conserving natural resources, reducing carbon emissions, and preserving natural habitats.

To address the growing concerns and fears of the general public, many environmental laws were enacted in the 1970s and 1980s. The National Environmental Policy Act, signed by then-President Richard Nixon in 1970, requires that before any programs are to begin, federal agencies must conduct a thorough assessment of their impact on the environment. Other important laws that help guide sustainable business practices as we know them today include the Federal Water Pollution Control Act, or Clean Water Act, (1972); the Safe Drinking Water Act (1974); the Toxic Substances Control Act (1976); Superfund legislation, known as the Comprehensive Environmental Response, Compensation, and Liability Act (CERCLA), which was passed to clean up hazardous-waste sites (1980); and the Emergency Planning and Community Right-To-Know Act (1986).

In the decades since, more companies have been hiring sustainability professionals to help them comply with environmental regulations and laws, as well as to prove to customers and the general public that they are a socially responsible operation.

THE JOB

Sustainability professionals work in any number of sectors for companies that are "greening" their businesses and/or have to adjust their operations to comply with environmental laws. Some companies hire *sustainability consultants* to work on a project-by-project basis, while other companies are creating sustainability offices and building staff teams to address issues of sustainability on a daily basis. Sustainability professionals may work for corporations and manufacturing companies, large and small businesses, nonprofit organizations, or even educational institutions. They may work as *management analysts*, hired to analyze the company's operations and identify areas of waste and inefficiency, and suggest and create plans for ways to function more sustainably.

Sustainability professionals may work for colleges and universities that are trying to "clean up their act" as well. Take, for example, the University of Chicago, which, in 2008, established a sustainability office to make all aspects of the school's operations more environmentally sustainable. Workers on the sustainability office team created a work plan to reduce the university's impact on the environment, get the word out on campus about sustainability issues, and encourage and advance intellectual debate and analysis of environmental issues. Employees in a sustainability office, such as the one at University of Chicago, might hold such positions as *sustainability director*, who liaises with other departments (from communications to finance) on sustainability issues, maps out plans to help the organization operate in a more environmentally friendly way, writes reports and makes presentations, and is also responsible for hiring and managing staff. A *sustainability program coordinator*, reporting to the *sustainability director*, helps coordinate the sustainability initiatives. The program coordinator's job responsibilities can be diverse. The University of Chicago listed the job responsibilities as follows:

> ✤ Assist in integrating sustainability principles and practices into the operational and academic functions of the university

❧ Develop ideas to advance the university's sustainability commitment; evaluate the ideas, analyzing for technical feasibility and cost effectiveness, and making sure the university community approves and accepts the ideas

❧ Create detailed implementation plans; work with units to implement approved project plans; and analyze effectiveness and results of projects

❧ Support the ongoing work of the Sustainability Council (a group comprised of faculty, academic personnel, students, and staff), as well as associated workgroups

❧ Engage student groups in the work of the Sustainability Office

❧ Research and analyze emerging environmental issues, keep abreast of sustainability initiatives at peer institutions, and assess feasibility of new technology on campus

❧ Help plan, coordinate, and implement activities developed by the Office and the Sustainability Council, including but not limited to seminars, conferences, workshops, and internships, that promote sustainability at the university and in the community at large

❧ Encourage and facilitate sustainability programs initiated by students, faculty, staff, and other community members

❧ Develop and implement other special projects that will advance the university's sustainability efforts, improve coordination among units across the campus, and raise awareness of sustainability-related projects being carried out in the neighborhood and surrounding community

❧ Assist in implementing a communications plan for university sustainability efforts; includes managing, creating materials for, and maintaining the sustainability Web site, and communicating successes and achievements in sustainability across the university to encourage increased participation

REQUIREMENTS
High School
To prepare for a career in this field, get a well-rounded education while in high school. Take science classes, including biology, chemistry, ecology, and earth science. Math, business, and English classes

will give you a good foundation for the business analysis, reports, and presentations you will work on once you are in the sustainability field. Take foreign language classes as well. Knowing another language is a plus as it will help you communicate with colleagues and clients from other countries, and can enhance your chances of finding work.

Postsecondary Training

An undergraduate degree is usually the minimum educational requirement for jobs in the sustainability industry. College majors vary depending on the job. Fields of study can include business, economics, engineering, forestry, green building and architecture, biology, or environmental science, to name only a few. Other helpful classes to take while in college include history, anthropology, English and communications, art, and design software programs (depending on field of interest). A graduate degree is typically required for upper-level management positions.

Certification or Licensing

Certification is not required, but it shows achievement of a level of technical expertise and industry knowledge that can help sustainability professionals advance in their careers. The Association of Energy Engineers (AEE) offers the Certified Sustainable Development Professional (CSDP) program to candidates who meet one of the following criteria:

- A four-year engineering or architectural degree from an accredited university or college, have a current professional engineer (PE) or similar status, and at least three years of experience in energy efficiency and pollution prevention, or sustainable development
- A four-year degree in business or related degree from an accredited university or college, with at least five years of experience in energy efficiency and pollution prevention, or sustainable development
- A two-year technical degree from an accredited college, with at least eight years of experience in energy efficiency and pollution prevention, or sustainable development
- Ten years or more of verified work experience in energy efficiency and pollution prevention, or sustainable development

Individuals who meet the pre-requisites must take the AEE training program and pass a four-hour exam to receive the CSDP designation.

Other Requirements
Solid communication skills are important for all jobs, regardless of specialty. The ability to write clear reports and present materials at meetings is essential. Curiosity, problem-solving skills, and the ability to work with a variety of people at all levels are also helpful in this field. Creative thinkers in particular thrive here, as many of the jobs require improving upon existing organizational operations. Detail-oriented individuals who are flexible, have an open mind, and possess a willingness to continually learn new things do well in this type of work.

EXPLORING
A great way to learn more about the sustainability field is to volunteer or work for a nonprofit organization. You can find internship and job listings, and learn more about opportunities in the industry by visiting such Web sites as Jobs in Sustainability (http://www.

Read All About It

Chiras, Dan. *Superbia! 31 Ways to Create More Sustainable Neighbourhoods*. Gabriola Island, BC, Canada: New Society Publishers, 2003.

Edwards, Andres R. *The Sustainability Revolution: Portrait of a Paradigm Shift*. Gabriola Island, BC, Canada: New Society Publishers, 2005.

Schendler, Auden. *Getting Green Done: Hard Truths from the Front Lines of the Sustainability Revolution*. Jackson, Tenn.: PublicAffairs, 2009.

Wheeler, Stephen. *Planning for Sustainability: Creating Livable, Equitable and Ecological Communities*. New York: Routledge, 2004.

Wilhelm, Kevin. *Return on Sustainability*. Indianapolis, Ind.: Dog Ear Publishing, 2009.

jobsinsustainability.com), Idealist (http://www.idealist.org), and Simply Hired (http://simplyhired.com).

EMPLOYERS

Sustainability professionals are employed by federal, state, and local governments; large and small businesses; colleges, universities, and public and private schools; corporations; manufacturers; and nonprofits. They work for organizations whose mission is to promote sustainability, and they work for companies that are trying to operate more sustainably. There are no specific statistics as of yet for the number of sustainability professionals employed in the field. You can get some idea of the numbers, however, from the following statistics: The U.S. Department of Labor cites that there were 678,000 management analysts and 247,000 administrative services managers employed in 2006.

STARTING OUT

Sustainability professionals start their careers in any number of ways. Some get their foot in the door by interning for a company while they are still in college, and then working their way up. For others, it may begin as a part-time job, which can lead to full-time opportunities down the road. You can find more information about sustainability careers and listings of events and resources by visiting the Web site of SustainableBusiness.com (http://sustainable business.com).

ADVANCEMENT

Advancement depends on the level of experience and the nature of the work. Junior sustainability professionals can advance by taking on more responsibilities and handling more complex projects. They may move up within the company to management positions. They may also start their own consulting companies. Writing and lecturing are other ways to expand in the sustainability field.

EARNINGS

Salaries for sustainability professionals vary widely depending upon the industry, the job specialty, and level of experience. According to the U.S. Department of Labor, general and operations managers earned median annual wages of $91,570 in 2008, with the lowest

Getting Your Feet Wet

Sometimes a first career step in the sustainability profession involves more than just dipping your toes in the water . . . literally. The Waterpod, a public art project created by artist Mary Mattingly, needed an intern in the fall of 2009 to literally hop on board the "floating, living sculpture" and get to work on a variety of tasks. The Waterpod traveled the waterways of the five New York City boroughs in the summer and fall of 2009. During that time, four artists lived aboard, using gardens, rainwater/greywater harvesting, solar power, chicken eggs, compost, and appropriate technologies to sustain themselves. People could visit The Waterpod for art events, and lectures on sustainability and environmental awareness. The intern they were seeking was someone who was studying, and passionate about, sustainable living and design (such as organic gardening, composting, rainwater catchment, hydroponics, etc.). A good attitude, the ability to maintain and improve the systems on the sculpture, and openness to learning more about them were key. The duties of the job entailed gardening, building furniture for the media centers on board, permaculture design, as well as giving tours to the public about the sustainability systems on board. Some construction experience was required, such as building structures, and helping with plumbing, drilling, and handyman situations. Benefits of the job also included meeting many leaders in the green/sustainability world, including scientists, engineers, professors, ecourbanist designers, and artists.

paid 10 percent earning $45,410 and the top paid 10 percent bringing in $137,020 or more. Salaries for administrative service managers ranged from $37,430 to $129,770 or higher in 2008. Administrative service managers who worked for colleges, universities, and professional schools had annual incomes of $78,940. Operations research analysts averaged $69,000 per year in 2008, with salaries starting at $40,000 and ranging up to $118,130 or more. Business management analysts brought home annual salaries ranging from $41,910 to upward of $133,850. Those who worked for management, scientific, and technical consulting services in 2008 averaged $96,420 per year. Federally employed management analysts had median annual incomes of $80,140, while those who worked for the state government averaged $56,480 per year.

In addition to salaries, sustainability professionals who are on staff may also receive benefits such as health and dental insurance, disability, paid vacations, holidays, sick leave, 401(k) plans, salary bonuses, and other incentives.

WORK ENVIRONMENT

Sustainability professionals work indoors in comfortable, well-lit offices in companies and in universities. Work hours are generally 40 hours per week, with more hours required when project deadlines are tightening. Some travel may be required for certain jobs, particularly for meetings, conferences, and lectures.

OUTLOOK

Job growth is expected to be decent for sustainability professionals in the next decade. Employment opportunities should continue to grow as more companies turn to sustainability professionals to help them meet federal and state environmental regulations, and to help them enhance their corporate social responsibility programs. The U.S. government continues to pass more environmental legislation concerning clean energy and technology, requiring companies to reduce carbon emissions and use fuel and other resources more efficiently. Sustainability professionals will be needed to advise on the best ways for businesses to operate with the least impact on the environment and on communities.

FOR MORE INFORMATION

For information on sustainability professional certification and other resources, visit the AEE Web site.

Association of Energy Engineers (AEE)
4025 Pleasantdale Road, Suite 420
Atlanta, GA 30340-4260
Tel: 770-447-5083
Email: info@aeecenter.org
http://www.aeecenter.org

For information about internships, career conferences, and publications, contact

Environmental Careers Organization
30 Winter Street, 6th Floor
Boston, MA 02108-4720

Tel: 480-515-2525
Email: admin@eco.org
http://www.eco.org

Learn more about sustainability practices and environmental policies and laws by visiting the EPA's Web site.
Environmental Protection Agency (EPA)
http://www.epa.gov

Find membership information, newsletters, Webinars, and more at
International Society of Sustainability Professionals
2515 NE 17th Avenue, Suite 300
Portland, OR 97212-4239
http://sustainabilityprofessionals.org

Wastewater Treatment Plant Operators and Technicians

QUICK FACTS

School Subjects
Chemistry
Mathematics

Personal Skills
Mechanical/manipulative
Technical/scientific

Work Environment
Indoors and outdoors
Primarily one location

Minimum Education Level
Some postsecondary training

Salary Range
$23,710 to $38,430 to
$59,860+

Certification or Licensing
Required in certain states

Outlook
Faster than the average

OVERVIEW

Wastewater treatment plant operators control, monitor, and maintain the equipment and treatment processes in wastewater (sewage) treatment plants. They remove or neutralize the chemicals, solid materials, and organisms in wastewater so that the water is not polluted when it is returned to the environment. There are approximately 111,000 water and liquid waste treatment plant operators currently working in the United States.

Wastewater treatment plant technicians work under the supervision of wastewater treatment plant operators. Technicians take samples and monitor treatment to ensure treated water is safe for its intended use. Depending on the level of treatment, water is used for human consumption or for nonconsumptive purposes, such as field irrigation or discharge into natural water sources. Some technicians also work in labs, where they collect and analyze water samples and maintain lab equipment.

HISTORY

Water systems and the disposal of wastes are ancient concerns. Thousands of years ago, the Minoans on the island of Crete built some of the earliest known domestic drainage systems. Later, the Romans created marvelous feats of engineering, including enclosed sewer lines that drained both rain runoff and water from the public baths. Urban sanitation methods, however, were limited. Garbage and human waste were collected from streets and homes and dumped into open watercourses leading away from the cities.

These processes changed little until the 19th century. The health hazards of contact with refuse were poorly understood, but as populations grew, disease outbreaks and noxious conditions in crowded areas made sanitation an important issue. Problems worsened with the industrial revolution, which led to both increased population concentrations and industrial wastes that required disposal.

Early efforts by sanitation engineers in the 19th century attempted to take advantage of natural processes. Moderate amounts of pollutants in flowing water go through a natural purification that gradually renders them less harmful. Operators of modern wastewater treatment plants monitor the process that does essentially the same thing that occurs naturally in rivers to purify water, only faster and more effectively. Today's plants are highly sophisticated, complex operations that may utilize biological processes, filtration, chemical treatments, and other methods of removing waste that otherwise may allow bacteria to colonize (live in) critical drinking supplies.

Wastewater treatment operators and technicians must comply with stringent government standards for removing pollutants. Under the Federal Water Pollution Control Act of 1972 and later reauthorizations, it is illegal to discharge any pollutant into the environment without a permit. Industries that send wastes to municipal treatment plants must meet minimum standards and pretreat the wastes so they do not damage the treatment facilities. Standards are also imposed on the treatment plants, controlling the quality of the water they discharge into rivers, streams, and the ocean.

THE JOB

Wastewater from homes, public buildings, and industrial plants is transported through sewer pipes to treatment plants. The wastes include both organic and inorganic substances, some of which may be highly toxic, such as lead and mercury. Wastewater treatment plant operators and technicians regulate the flow of incoming wastewater by adjusting pumps, valves, and other equipment, either manually or through remote controls. They keep track of the various meters and gauges that monitor the purification processes and indicate how the equipment is operating. Using the information from these instruments, they control the pumps, engines, and generators that move the untreated water through the processes of filtration, settling, aeration, and sludge digestion. They also operate chemical-feeding devices, collect water samples, and perform laboratory tests, so that the proper level of chemicals, such as chlorine, is maintained in the wastewater. Technicians may record instrument readings and other information in logs of plant operations. These logs are supervised and monitored by operators. Computers are commonly used to monitor and regulate wastewater treatment equipment and processes. Specialized software allows operators to store and analyze data, which is particularly useful when something in the system malfunctions.

The duties of operators and technicians vary somewhat with the size and type of plant where they work. In small plants one person per shift may be able to do all the necessary routine tasks. But in larger plants, there may be a number of operators, each specializing in just a few activities and working as part of a team that includes engineers, chemists, technicians, mechanics, helpers, and other employees. Some facilities are equipped to handle both wastewater treatment and treatment of the clean water supplied to municipal water systems, and plant operators may be involved with both functions.

Other routine tasks that plant operators and technicians perform include maintenance and minor repairs on equipment such as valves and pumps. They may use common hand tools such as wrenches and pliers and special tools adapted specifically for the equipment. In large facilities, they also direct attendants and helpers who take care of some routine tasks and maintenance work. The accumulated residues of wastes from the water must be removed from the plant, and operators may dispose of these materials. Some of this final product, or sludge, can be reclaimed for uses such as soil conditioners or fuel for the production of electricity.

A wastewater treatment plant superintendent must supervise all of the operations carried out at the facility. *AP Photo/The Herald-Sun, William F. West*

Technicians may also survey streams and study basin areas to determine water availability. To assist the engineers they work with, technicians prepare graphs, tables, sketches, and diagrams to illustrate survey data. They file plans and documents, answer public inquiries, help train new personnel, and perform various other support duties.

Plant operators and technicians sometimes have to work under emergency conditions, such as when heavy rains flood the sewer pipes, straining the treatment plant's capacity, or when there is a chlorine gas leak or oxygen deficiency in the treatment tanks. When a serious problem arises, they must work quickly and effectively to solve it as soon as possible.

REQUIREMENTS
High School
A high school diploma or its equivalent is required for a job as a wastewater treatment plant operator or technician, and additional specialized technical training is generally preferred for both

positions. A desirable background for this work includes high school courses in chemistry, biology, mathematics, and computers; welding or electrical training may be helpful as well. Other characteristics that employers look for include mechanical aptitude and the ability to perform mathematical computations easily. You should be able to solve basic algebra and statistics problems. Future technicians may be required to prepare reports containing statistics and other scientific documentation. Communications, statistics, and algebra are useful for this career path; such courses enable the technician to prepare graphs, tables, sketches, and diagrams to illustrate surveys for the operators and engineers they support.

Postsecondary Training

As treatment plants become more technologically complex, workers who have previous training in the field are increasingly at an advantage. Specialized education in wastewater technology is available in two-year programs that lead to an associate's degree and one-year programs that lead to a certificate. Such programs, which are offered at some community and junior colleges and vocational-technical institutes, provide a good general knowledge of water pollution control and will prepare you to become an operator or technician. Beginners must still learn the details of operations at the plant where they work, but their specialized training increases their chances for better positions and later promotions.

Many operators and technicians acquire the skills they need during a period of on-the-job training. Newly hired workers often begin as attendants or operators-in-training. Working under the supervision of experienced operators, they pick up knowledge and skills by observing other workers and by doing routine tasks such as recording meter readings, collecting samples, and general cleaning and plant maintenance. In larger plants, trainees may study supplementary written material provided at the plant, or they may attend classes in which they learn plant operations.

Wastewater treatment plant operators and technicians often have various opportunities to continue learning about their field. Most state water pollution control agencies offer training courses for people employed in the field. Subjects covered by these training courses include principles of treatment processes and process control, odors and their control, safety, chlorination, sedimentation, biological oxidation, sludge treatment and disposal, and flow measurements. Correspondence courses on related subject areas also are available. Some employers help pay tuition for workers who take related college-level courses in science or engineering.

Certification or Licensing

Workers who control operations at wastewater treatment plants must be certified by most states. To obtain certification, operators must pass an examination given by the state. There is no nationwide standard, so different states administer different tests. Many states issue several classes of certification, depending on the size of the plant the worker is qualified to control. Certification may be beneficial even if it is not a requirement and no matter how much experience a worker already has. In Illinois, for example, operators who have the minimum state certification level are automatically

More People, Less Water

Recycling things such as aluminum cans, paper, and glass is a great way to help preserve our environment. But many of us don't think about the importance of recycling one of our most important renewable resources—water. Water is something we have been recycling for years. It is an ideal recyclable because it is never used up. Every glass of water you drink contains water molecules that have been used countless times before, perhaps in someone else's glass of water, a swimming pool, or even a fire hydrant. That's why wastewater treatment plants are so important—they make sure the water you drink is clean and safe, no matter where it's been.

As the world's population grows, wastewater treatment plants will become more important to our environment because the supply of cheap, easily available water will shrink. Even in the United States, which as a nation has plenty of fresh water, groundwater is being used at a rate 25 percent higher than its replenishment rate. Areas with fast-growing populations and limited water supplies, such as parts of California, Florida, and Texas, face the highest risk for water shortages in the 21st century. Conserving water in those areas by finding new ways to use less water and make better use of the water we have is something that can be done now. Using effluent (partially treated water) for nonconsumptive purposes, such as irrigation of golf courses, is something that's being done in California, Florida, and the southwestern United States. This is a good example of how wastewater treatment plants are vital tools for conserving our environment.

eligible for higher pay than those without any certification, although certification is not a requirement of employment.

Other Requirements

Operators and technicians must be familiar with the provisions of the Federal Clean Water Act and various state and local regulations that apply to their work. Whenever they become responsible for more complex processes and equipment, they must become acquainted with a wider scope of guidelines and regulations. In larger cities and towns especially, job applicants may have to take a civil service exam or other tests that assess their aptitudes and abilities.

EXPLORING

See if you can arrange to visit a wastewater treatment plant to observe its operations. It can also be helpful to investigate courses and requirements of any programs in wastewater technology or environmental resources programs offered by a local technical school or college. Part-time or summer employment as a helper in a wastewater treatment plant could be a very helpful experience, but such a job may be hard to find. A job in any kind of machine shop may be easier to come by, and can provide you with an opportunity to become familiar with handling machinery and common tools.

Ask wastewater plant operators or technicians in your city if you can interview them about their jobs. Learning about water conservation and water quality in general can be useful. Government agencies or citizen groups dedicated to improving water quality or conserving water can educate you about water quality and supply in your area.

EMPLOYERS

About 80 percent of the approximately 111,000 wastewater treatment plant operators in the United States are employed by local governments; others work for the federal government, utility companies, or private sanitary services that operate under contracts with local governments. Jobs are located throughout the country, with the greatest numbers found in areas with high populations.

Wastewater treatment plant operators and technicians can find jobs with state or federal water pollution control agencies, where they monitor plants and provide technical assistance. Examples of such agencies are the Army Corps of Engineers and the

Environmental Protection Agency. These jobs normally require vocational-technical school or community college training. Other experienced wastewater workers find employment with industrial wastewater treatment plants, companies that sell wastewater treatment equipment and chemicals, large utilities, consulting firms, or vocational-technical schools.

STARTING OUT

Graduates of most postsecondary technical programs and some high schools can get help in locating job openings from the career services office of the school they attended. Another source of information is the local office of the state employment service. Job seekers may also directly contact state and local water pollution control agencies and the personnel offices of wastewater treatment facilities in desired locations.

In some plants, a person must first work as a wastewater treatment plant technician before becoming an operator or working in a supervisory position. Wastewater treatment plant technicians have many of the same duties as a plant operator but less responsibility. They inspect, study, and sample existing water treatment systems and evaluate new structures for efficacy and safety. Support work and instrumentation reading make up the bulk of the technician's day.

Use the Internet to find job leads. Professional associations, such as the Water Environment Federation (http://www.wef.org), offer job listings in the wastewater field as part of their Web site. Such sites are good resources for someone getting started in the field, as they also list available internship or trainee positions. Also, an Internet search using the words "wastewater treatment plant operator or technician" will generate a list of Web sites that may contain job postings and internship opportunities.

ADVANCEMENT

As operators gain skills and experience, they are assigned tasks that involve more responsibility for more complex activities. Some technicians advance to become operators. Some operators advance to become *plant supervisors* or *plant superintendents*. The qualifications that superintendents need are related to the size and complexity of the plant. In smaller plants, experienced operators with some postsecondary training may be promoted to superintendent positions. In larger plants, educational requirements are increasing along with the sophistication and complexity of their systems, and superintendents usually have bachelor's degrees in engineering or science.

Some operators and technicians advance by transferring to a related job. Such jobs may require additional schooling or training to specialize in water pollution control, commercial wastewater equipment sales, or teaching wastewater treatment in a vocational or technical school.

Profile: Fred Kloepper

More than 10 years ago, Fred Kloepper of Bakersfield, California, made a career change. He was an accomplished civil engineer with the Kern County and Bakersfield Public Works Department, having contributed to highway and bridge design, office engineering, construction inspection, and airport design. His experience with wastewater treatment had been limited until that time, and he wanted to change that. His civil engineering duties came to include assignments in the sanitary field. He liked this work and decided to specialize in wastewater treatment. Today, he reports high satisfaction with his job. He is the wastewater manager, overseeing two plants with nine wastewater treatment operators. "It's kind of a strange thing. It's a field with very little turnover," he says. "We operate two medium-sized plants with nine operators and two laboratory technicians, and we have had no operator turnover since I've been here. People don't leave this field for another field; generally, the only turnover we have is retirement."

Kloepper has found wastewater treatment a challenging and rewarding career. He was selected by the American Public Works Association as one of the top 10 public works employees in the nation in 1997. In part, this recognition came for his work in getting the state of California to reclassify sludge from one of Bakersfield's treatment plants to nonhazardous, saving the city (and taxpayers) thousands of dollars and preserving a cost-efficient fertilizer for farmers. He believes in the importance of conserving water and oversees efforts to reuse effluent (water that has gone through secondary treatment at a wastewater treatment plant) to irrigate nonhuman consumption crops, such as feed corn, fibers, and alfalfa.

EARNINGS

Salaries of wastewater treatment plant operators and technicians vary depending on factors such as the size of the plant, the workers' job responsibilities, and their level of certification. According to the U.S. Department of Labor, water and liquid waste treatment plant operators earned median annual salaries of $38,430 in 2008. The lowest paid 10 percent earned $23,710 or less, while the highest paid 10 percent earned $59,860 or more a year. In local government, plant operators earned a median salary of $40,020 in 2008.

In addition to their pay, most operators and technicians receive benefits such as life and health insurance, a pension plan, and reimbursement for education and training related to their job.

WORK ENVIRONMENT

In small towns, plant operators may only work part time or may handle other duties as well as wastewater treatment. The size and type of plant also determine the range of duties. In larger plants with many employees, operators and technicians usually perform more specialized functions. In some cases, they may be responsible for monitoring only a single process. In smaller plants, workers likely will have a broader range of responsibilities. Wastewater treatment plants operate 24 hours a day, every day of the year. Operators and technicians usually work one of three eight-hour shifts, often on a rotating basis so that employees share the evening and night work. Overtime is often required during emergencies.

The work takes operators and technicians both indoors and outdoors. They must contend with noisy machinery and may have to tolerate unpleasant odors, despite the use of chlorine and other chemicals to control odors. The job involves moving about, stooping, reaching, and climbing. Operators and technicians often get their clothes dirty. Slippery sidewalks, dangerous gases, and malfunctioning equipment are potential hazards of the job, but workers can minimize their risk of injury by following safety guidelines.

OUTLOOK

The future looks good for wastewater treatment plant operators and technicians. Employment in this field is expected to grow faster than the average for all occupations through 2016. The number of job applicants in this field is generally low due to the unclean and physically demanding nature of the work. Also, the growth in demand for wastewater treatment will be related to the overall growth of the nation's population and economy. As the population increases, new treatment plants will be built to meet need, and existing ones will be upgraded, requiring additional trained personnel to manage their operations. Other openings will arise when experienced workers retire or transfer to new occupations. Operators and technicians with formal training will have the best chances for attaining new positions and promotions.

Workers in wastewater treatment plants are rarely laid off, even during a recession, because wastewater treatment is essential to public health and welfare. In the future more wastewater professionals will probably be employed by private companies that contract to manage treatment plants for local governments.

FOR MORE INFORMATION

For current information on the field of wastewater management, contact

American Water Works Association
6666 West Quincy Avenue
Denver, CO 80235-3098
Tel: 303-794-7711
http://www.awwa.org

For environmental job listings, contact

Environmental Careers Organization
Tel: 480-515-2525
Email: admin@eco.org
http://www.eco.org

**National Environmental, Safety, and Health Training
  Association**
PO Box 10321
Phoenix, AZ 85064-0321
Tel: 602-956-6099
Email: neshta@neshta.org
http://www.neshta.org

For career information, contact or visit the following Web site:

Water Environment Federation
601 Wythe Street
Alexandria, VA 22314-1994
Tel: 800-666-0206
http://www.wef.org

Further Reading

Aubrey, Sarah B. *Starting & Running Your Own Small Farm Business.* North Adams, Mass.: Storey Publishing, 2008.

Barnes, Burton V. et al. *Forest Ecology.* 4th ed. Hoboken, N.J.: Wiley, 1998.

Beebe, William. *The Book of Naturalists.* Princeton, N.J.: Princeton University Press, 1988.

Beidleman, Richard G. *California's Frontier Naturalists.* Berkeley, Calif.: University of California Press, 2006.

Blackburn, William R. *The Sustainability Handbook: The Complete Management Guide to Achieving Social, Economic and Environmental Responsibility.* London, England: Earthscan Publications, 2007.

Borghesi, Simone, and Alessandro Vercelli. *Global Sustainability: Social and Environmental Conditions.* New York: Palgrave Macmillan, 2008.

Byczynski, Lynn. *Market Farming Success.* Lawrence, Kan.: Fairplain Publications, 2006.

Corum, Vance et al. *The New Farmers' Market: Farm-Fresh Ideas for Producers, Managers & Communities.* Auburn, Calif.: New World Publishing, 2005.

Cutright, Paul Russell, and Paul A. Johnsgard. *Lewis and Clark: Pioneering Naturalists.* 2d ed. Winnipeg, Canada: Bison Books, 2003.

Dresner, Simon. *The Principles of Sustainability.* London, England: Earthscan Publications Ltd., 2002.

Fossel, Peter V. *Organic Farming: Everything You Need to Know.* Osceola, Wis.: Voyageur Press, 2007.

Fromartz, Samuel. *Organic, Inc.: Natural Foods and How They Grew.* Fort Washington, Pa.: Harvest Books, 2007.

Grosz, Terry. *A Sword for Mother Nature: The Further Adventures of a Fish and Game Warden.* Boulder, Colo.: Johnson Books, 2002.

Huffstodt, Jim. *Everglades Lawmen: True Stories of Game Wardens in the Glades.* Sarasota, Fla.: Pineapple Press, 2000.

Huxley, Robert. *The Great Naturalists.* London, England: Thames & Hudson, 2007.

Kresic, Neven. *Groundwater Resources: Sustainability, Management, and Restoration.* New York: McGraw-Hill Professional, 2008.

Kross, Katie. *Profession and Purpose: A Resource Guide for MBA Careers in Sustainability.* Sheffield, England: Greenleaf Publishing, 2009.

Liu, Cheng. *Soil Properties: Testing, Measurement, and Evaluation.* 6th ed. Upper Saddle River, N.J.: Prentice Hall, 2008.

Mays, Larry W. *Water Resources Engineering.* Hoboken, N.J.: Wiley, 2004.

McCarthy, David. *Essentials of Soil Mechanics and Foundations: Basic Geotechnics.* 7th ed. Upper Saddle River, N.J.: Prentice Hall, 2006.

Metcalf & Eddy, Inc. *Water Reuse: Issues, Technologies, and Applications.* New York: McGraw-Hill Professional, 2007.

Munier, Nolberto. *Handbook on Urban Sustainability.* New York: Springer, 2007.

Munier, Nolberto. *Introduction to Sustainability: Road to a Better Future.* New York: Springer, 2009.

Nazaroff, William W., and Lisa Alvarez-Cohen. *Environmental Engineering Science.* Hoboken, N.J.: Wiley, 2000.

Perry, David A. et al. *Forest Ecosystems.* 2d ed. Baltimore, Md.: The Johns Hopkins University Press, 2008.

Robinson, Jennifer Meta, and J.A. Hartenfeld. *The Farmers' Market Book: Growing Food, Cultivating Community.* Beverly, Mass.: Quarry Books, 2007.

Ronald, Pamela C., and R.W. Adamchak. *Tomorrow's Table: Organic Farming, Genetics, and the Future of Food.* New York: Oxford University Press, 2008.

Sibley, David Allen. *The Sibley Guide to Trees.* New York: Knopf, 2009.

Spellman, Frank R. *Handbook of Water and Wastewater Treatment Plant Operations.* 2d ed. New York: CRC Press, 2006.

Steger, Ulrich. *Sustainability Partnerships: The Manager's Handbook.* New York: Palgrave Macmillan, 2009.

Stewart, Keith. *It's a Long Road to a Tomato: Tales of an Organic Farmer Who Quit the Big City for the (Not So) Simple Life.* Cambridge, Mass.: Da Capo Press, 2006.

Tangires, Helen. *Public Markets and Civic Culture in Nineteenth-Century America.* Baltimore: Johns Hopkins University Press, 2003.

Tchobanoglous, George, and H. David Stensel. *Wastewater Engineering: Treatment and Resuse.* New York: McGraw-Hill Science/Engineering/Math, 2002.

Todd, David Keith. *Groundwater Hydrology.* 3d ed. Hoboken, N.J.: Wiley, 2008.

Unger, Paul. *Soil and Water Conservation Handbook: Policies, Practices, Conditions, and Terms.* New York: CRC Press, 2006.

Uphoff, Norman et al, eds. *Biological Approaches to Sustainable Soil Systems.* New York: CRC Press, 2006.

Water Environmental Federation. *Operation of Municipal Wastewater Treatment Plants: Manual of Practice 11.* New York: McGraw-Hill Professional, 2007.

Wille, Christopher. *Opportunities in Forestry Careers.* New York: McGraw-Hill, 2003.

Wiswall, Richard. *The Organic Farmer's Business Handbook: A Complete Guide to Managing Finances, Crops, and Staff – and Making a Profit.* White River Junction, Vt.: Chelsea Green Publishing, 2009.

The World Bank. *Sustainable Land Management: Challenges, Opportunities, and Trade-Offs (Agriculture and Rural Development).* Washington, D.C.: World Bank Publications, 2006.

Index

Entries and page numbers in **bold** indicate major treatment of a topic.